simply sweet
COLORCAKES

Oxmoor House

welcome!

Whether bright and bold, rainbow-hued, swirled, or tie-dyed, **Simply Sweet ColorCakes** makes dessert more fun with fantastic colors! Prepare to be wowed with more than 125 dipped, sprinkled, layered, stacked, and on-a-stick sweet treats that can be easily made at home.

Surprise and delight the kid in everyone with bakery-worthy confections made simple to create. From beautiful images that inspire, to step-by-step photo tutorials for perfect results every time, it's easy to make any of these fanciful treats.

Clever "Color Wow" tip boxes give ideas for taking each look to the next level or swapping out color combinations. Helpful "Simply Smart" tips share secrets for making recipes even easier. Now you can get that stunning bakery look for cakes, cookies, cupcakes, bars, and frozen treats right in your own kitchen.

Simply Sweet ColorCakes is all about cute, clever, whimsical, and great-tasting treats that anyone can make—perfect for celebrations, school events, weekend get-togethers, and much more. Each tantalizing treat is so impressive, your friends will be asking, "How do you do that!?"

sweets on a stick

Step 3

Step 4

Step 4

rainbow cake pops

MAKES 32 CAKE POPS Hands-On Time: 50 min. Total Time: 3 hours, 55 min.

Paper baking cups

Cooking spray

1 (16.25-oz.) package white cake mix

Water, vegetable oil, and eggs called
    for on cake mix box

⅛ tsp. yellow food coloring paste

⅛ tsp. purple food coloring paste

⅛ tsp. orange food coloring paste

⅛ tsp. blue food coloring paste

⅛ tsp. green food coloring paste

¼ tsp. red food coloring paste

Parchment paper

¾ cup whipped ready-to-spread
    white frosting

32 (4-inch) paper lollipop sticks

1 (12-oz.) bag blue candy melts,
    melted

1½ cups each red, orange, yellow,
    green, blue, and purple candy
    melts, melted

Block of plastic foam

½ cup each red, orange, yellow,
    green, blue, and purple sanding
    sugar

1. Preheat oven to 350°. Place paper baking cups in 2 (12-cup) muffin pans; coat with cooking spray. Prepare cake mix according to package directions, using water, oil, and eggs. Divide batter evenly among 6 small bowls. Add one of each food coloring paste to each bowl, and mix well.

2. Spoon each color batter into 4 muffin cups, filling two-thirds full. Bake at 350° for 18 to 20 minutes or until a wooden pick inserted in center comes out clean. Cool in pans on wire racks 10 minutes; remove from pans to wire racks, and cool completely (about 20 minutes).

3. Line bottom and sides of an 8- x 4-inch loaf pan with parchment or wax paper, allowing 1 to 2 inches to extend over sides. Crumble purple cupcakes into a small bowl. Add 2 Tbsp. frosting, and mix until a soft dough forms. Press dough evenly into bottom of loaf pan. Repeat with blue, green, yellow, orange, and red cupcakes and remaining frosting in that order. Cover and chill 2 hours or until firm.

4. Use parchment paper to lift cake out of loaf pan. Cut cake into 32 squares; roll each square into a ball. Place on a parchment paper-lined baking sheet. Dip tip of 1 lollipop stick ½ inch into melted blue candy, and insert stick halfway into 1 cake ball. Repeat with remaining sticks and cake balls; chill 15 minutes. Remove several cake balls from refrigerator at a time. Working 1 at a time, dip cake balls into various melted colored candy to coat. Gently tap off excess, and poke opposite ends of sticks into foam block. Sprinkle pops with corresponding colored sugar. Let stand until set.

bluebird cake pops

MAKES 48 CAKE POPS   Hands-On Time: 2 hours, 20 min.   Total Time: 3 hours, 50 min.

These perky little birdies are perfect for a springtime party. Run parchment paper through a paper shredder to make a nest for your flock!

1 (18.25-oz.) package milk chocolate
    cake mix
Water, vegetable oil, and eggs called
    for on cake mix box
Wax paper
1 cup whipped ready-to-spread
    buttercream frosting
16 (0.55-oz.) packages blue raspberry
    taffy candies
½ oz. neon orange fondant (from
    17.6-oz. box assorted neon colors)
4½ tsp. shortening
¾ tsp. blue candy color (oil-based)
3 cups blue candy melts, melted
    (18 oz.)
48 paper lollipop sticks
Block of plastic foam
Small black confetti candies

1. Preheat oven to 350°. Prepare and bake cake mix according to package directions for 13- x 9-inch pan, using water, oil, and eggs. Cool completely.

2. Line a baking sheet with wax paper. Crumble cake into a large bowl. Add frosting; mix well. Shape into 48 (1¼-inch) oblong balls; pinch narrow ends to look like tail feathers. Place on baking sheet. Freeze until firm; when firm, transfer to refrigerator.

3. With kitchen scissors, cut taffy candies into wing shapes. Shape fondant into 48 (¼-inch) cones for beaks. Stir shortening and candy color into melted candy until smooth. Dip tip of 1 lollipop stick about ½ inch into melted candy; insert stick no more than halfway into 1 cake ball. Repeat with remaining sticks and cake balls. Return pops to baking sheet. Chill 5 minutes.

4. Remove a few cake balls at a time, and dip each cake ball into melted candy to coat; gently tap off excess. Poke opposite ends of sticks into foam block. Immediately attach wings, confetti for eyes, and orange cone for beak. Let stand until set.

strawberries-and-cream cake pops

MAKES 36 CAKE POPS   Hands-On Time: 40 min.   Total Time: 2 hours, 10 min.

1 (18.25-oz.) package white cake mix

Water, vegetable oil, and egg whites called for on cake mix box

Wax paper

½ cup powdered sugar

2 oz. cream cheese, softened

¼ cup butter, softened

¼ cup strawberry jam

1 cup dried strawberries, chopped

1 cup red candy melts, melted

2 (12-oz.) bags pink candy melts, melted

36 paper lollipop sticks

Block of plastic foam

½ cup pink decorator sugar crystals, pink jimmies, or pink and white sprinkles.

1. Preheat oven to 350°. Prepare and bake cake mix according to package directions for 13- x 9-inch pan, using water, oil, and egg whites. Cool completely.

2. Line a baking sheet with wax paper. In a large bowl, beat powdered sugar, cream cheese, butter, and jam at medium speed with an electric mixer until blended. Crumble cake into cream cheese mixture; mix well. Stir in dried strawberries. Shape into 36 (2-inch) balls; place on baking sheet. Freeze until firm. When cake balls are firm, transfer to refrigerator.

3. Spoon about 2 Tbsp. melted red candy into melted pink candy; swirl gently. Remove several cake balls from refrigerator at a time. Dip tip of 1 lollipop stick about ½ inch into melted candy, and insert stick into 1 cake ball no more than halfway. Repeat with remaining sticks and cake balls. Dip each cake ball into swirled candy to coat; gently tap off excess. (Spoon more red candy into pink candy as needed.) Poke opposite ends of sticks into foam block. Sprinkle with pink sugar crystals, jimmies, or sprinkles.

color wow!

Give these pops a graphic look by dipping them half in red candy melts and half in pink instead of swirling the colors.

school of fish cake pops

MAKES 54 CAKE POPS   Hands-On Time: 1 hour, 35 min.   Total Time: 4 hours, 20 min.

These pucker-faced pops are swimmingly delicious! Fill a bowl with raw sugar to place pops in—looks just like beach sand!

1 (18.25-oz.) package yellow cake mix

Water, vegetable oil, and eggs called for on cake mix box

Wax paper

1 cup whipped ready-to-spread white frosting

2 cups purple candy melts, melted

2 cups green candy melts, melted

2 cups orange candy melts, melted

3 Tbsp. shortening

54 paper lollipop sticks

Purple, green, and orange sanding sugar

54 pieces fruity O-shaped cereal

Small black confetti candies

Block of plastic foam

1. Preheat oven to 350°. Prepare and bake cake mix according to package directions for 13- × 9-inch pan, using water, oil, and eggs. Cool completely.

2. Line 2 baking sheets with wax paper. Crumble cake into large bowl. Add frosting; mix well. Shape into 54 (1¼-inch) balls; place on 1 baking sheet. Freeze until firm; transfer to refrigerator.

3. In 3 separate bowls, stir each color melted candy and 1 Tbsp. shortening until smooth. Spoon ¼ cup of each color candy into zip-top plastic freezer bags; seal bags. Cut off small corner of each bag; squeeze bags to pipe fish fins onto prepared baking sheet. Chill 5 minutes.

4. Dip tip of 1 lollipop stick about ½ inch into melted candy, and insert stick into 1 cake ball no more than halfway. Return to baking sheet. Chill 5 minutes. Remove from refrigerator 1 at a time. Dip cake ball into melted candy to coat; gently tap off excess. Coat with sanding sugar. Immediately attach candy fins, cereal for mouth, and confetti for eyes. Poke opposite end of stick into foam block. Let stand until set.

Step 2

Step 3

Step 4

cookies-and-cream cake pops

MAKES 84 CAKE POPS   Hands-On Time: 50 min.   Total Time: 2 hours, 30 min.

These pops pack a yummy surprise of cookies-and-cream on the inside. Make the outside coating any color you like and serve in mini cupcake wrappers.

1 (18.25-oz.) package white cake mix

Water, vegetable oil, and egg whites called for on cake mix box

Wax paper

12 cream-filled chocolate sandwich cookies, crushed (1 cup)

1 cup whipped ready-to-spread cream cheese frosting

84 paper lollipop sticks

2 cups green candy melts, melted

2 large blocks of plastic foam

2 cups blue candy melts, melted

2 cups yellow candy melts, melted

3/4 cup white chocolate morsels

2 Tbsp. coarse white sparkling sugar

1. Preheat oven to 350°. Prepare and bake cake mix according to package directions for 13- x 9-inch pan, using water, oil, and egg whites. Cool completely.

2. Line 2 baking sheets with wax paper. Crumble cake into large bowl. Add crushed cookies and frosting; mix well. Shape into 84 (1-inch) balls; place on baking sheets. Freeze about 15 minutes. When firm, transfer to refrigerator.

3. Remove one-third of cake balls from refrigerator. Dip tip of 1 lollipop stick ½ inch into melted green candy, and insert stick into 1 cake ball no more than halfway.

4. Dip cake ball into melted green candy to coat; gently tap off excess. Poke opposite end of stick into foam block. Repeat with remaining cake balls, coating one-third with blue candy and one-third with yellow candy.

5. Place white morsels in small zip-top plastic freezer bag; seal bag. Microwave at HIGH about 1 minute or until softened. Gently squeeze bag until chocolate is smooth; cut off tiny corner of bag. Squeeze bag to drizzle melted morsels over cake pops. Immediately sprinkle with sparkling sugar.

soft-serve cake pops

MAKES 12 CAKE POPS   Hands-On Time: 1 hour   Total Time: 3 hours, 20 min.

1 (18.25-oz.) package strawberry, chocolate, or vanilla cake mix

Water, vegetable oil, and eggs called for on cake mix box

Wax paper

1 cup whipped ready-to-spread strawberry frosting

12 flat-bottom ice-cream cones

12 oz. almond bark candy coating, melted

1½ cups rainbow candy sprinkles

Disposable decorating bag

1 (12-oz.) container whipped ready-to-spread vanilla frosting

1. Preheat oven to 350°. Prepare and bake cake mix according to package directions for 13- x 9-inch pan, using water, oil, and eggs. Cool completely (about 1 hour).

2. Line a baking sheet with wax paper. Crumble cake into large bowl. Add strawberry frosting; mix well. Roll into 12 (2-inch) balls; place on baking sheet. Chill until firm. Set remaining cake mixture aside.

3. Dip sides of cones in 1 cup melted candy; gently tap off excess. Dip in 1 cup sprinkles. Let stand until set.

4. Fill cones with reserved cake mixture. Reheat remaining candy in microwave, if necessary. Dip bottoms of cake balls into candy; place on top of cones. Let stand until set.

5. Insert a star tip into a large decorating bag; fill with vanilla frosting. Pipe frosting in 3 rotations around each cake ball, ending in small peak. Sprinkle tops with remaining ½ cup candy sprinkles.

color wow!

Ice-cream cones can be found in many colors. Pump up the color in these cake pops by using pink, flat-bottom ice-cream cones.

baby block cake pops

MAKES 42 CAKE POPS   Hands-On Time: 2 hours, 55 min.   Total Time: 5 hours, 40 min.

Tied up with a bow in pink or blue, these pops are sure to make guests swoon at a baby shower or christening.

1 (18.25-oz.) package white cake mix

Water, vegetable oil, and egg whites called for on cake mix box

Wax paper

1 cup ready-to-spread cream cheese frosting

1 cup pink candy melts, melted

1 cup yellow candy melts, melted

1 cup blue candy melts, melted

6 tsp. shortening

42 paper lollipop sticks

Block of plastic foam

1 (7-oz.) pouch white decorating cookie icing

1. Preheat oven to 350°. Prepare and bake cake mix according to package directions for 13- x 9-inch pan, using water, oil, and egg whites. Cool completely.

2. Line a baking sheet with wax paper. Crumble cake into large bowl. Add frosting; mix well. Shape into 42 (1-inch) cubes; place on baking sheet. Freeze until firm; transfer to refrigerator.

3. In 3 separate bowls, stir each color melted candy and 2 tsp. shortening until smooth. Dip tips of 14 of the lollipop sticks about ½ inch into melted pink candy, and insert each stick into 1 cake square no more than halfway. Repeat, dipping 14 sticks in yellow candy and 14 in blue. Return to baking sheet. Chill 20 minutes. Remove from refrigerator a few at a time. Dip each cake square into melted candy to coat (using same color to match stick); gently tap off excess. Poke opposite end of stick into foam block. Let stand until set.

4. On 1 side of each square, pipe white icing to look like a block. Pipe letter A, B, or C within each outline. Let stand until set.

citrus-poppy seed cake pops

MAKES 64 CAKE POPS   Hands-On Time: 1 hour, 10 min.   Total Time: 2 hours, 50 min.

1 (18.25-oz.) package lemon cake mix

Water, vegetable oil, and eggs called for on cake mix box

Wax paper

1 cup ready-to-spread vanilla frosting

3 Tbsp. poppy seeds, divided

2 tsp. orange zest

2 cups yellow candy melts

2 Tbsp. shortening

2 cups orange candy melts

64 paper lollipop sticks

Block of plastic foam

1. Preheat oven to 350°. Prepare and bake cake mix according to package directions for 13- x 9-inch pan, using water, oil, and eggs. Cool completely.

2. Line a baking sheet with wax paper. Crumble cake into large bowl. Add frosting, 2 Tbsp. poppy seeds, and orange zest; mix well. Shape into 64 (1-inch) balls; place on baking sheet. Freeze until firm; transfer to refrigerator.

3. In microwave-safe bowl, heat yellow candy melts and 1 Tbsp. shortening, uncovered, at MEDIUM (50% power) 1 minute, then in 15-second intervals until melted; stir until smooth. Repeat with orange candy melts and remaining 1 Tbsp. shortening. Dip tip of 1 lollipop stick about ½ inch into melted candy, and insert stick into 1 cake ball no more than halfway. Repeat with remaining sticks and cake balls, alternating color. Return to baking sheet. Chill 5 minutes. Remove from refrigerator a few at a time. Dip half of cake balls into yellow candy and half into orange candy; gently tap off excess. Poke opposite ends of sticks into foam block. Sprinkle tops with remaining 1 Tbsp. poppy seeds. Let stand until set.

just ducky lemonade cake pops

MAKES 36 CAKE POPS   Hands-On Time: 1 hour, 5 min.   Total Time: 2 hours, 30 min.

1 (15.25-oz.) package lemon cake mix

Water, vegetable oil, and eggs called for on cake mix box

Wax paper

1 cup plus 1 Tbsp. whipped ready-to-spread frosting, divided

3 Tbsp. presweetened lemonade-flavor drink mix

10 (0.55-oz.) packages yellow taffy candies

1/4 cup red fondant

4 cups yellow candy melts

2 Tbsp. shortening

36 paper lollipop sticks

Block of plastic foam

Small black confetti candies

Black jimmies

1. Preheat oven to 350°. Prepare and bake cake mix according to package directions for 13- x 9-inch pan, using water, oil, and eggs. Cool completely.

2. Line a baking sheet with wax paper. Crumble cake into large bowl. Add 1 cup frosting and drink mix; mix well. Shape mixture into 36 (1¼-inch) oblong balls; pinch narrow ends to look like tail feathers. Place on baking sheet. Shape remaining mixture into 36 (¾-inch) balls; place on baking sheet. Freeze until firm; transfer to refrigerator.

3. With kitchen scissors, cut taffy candies into wing shapes. Shape fondant into 72 (¼-inch) petal shapes for beaks. In microwave-safe bowl, heat candy melts and shortening, uncovered, at MEDIUM (50% power) for 2 minutes, stirring once, then in 15-second intervals until melted; stir until smooth. Dip tip of 1 lollipop stick about ½ inch into melted candy; insert stick no more than halfway into 1 oblong cake ball. Repeat with remaining lollipop sticks and oblong cake balls. Spread a small amount of melted candy on top of cake pop; attach 1 small cake ball to each. Return pops to baking sheet. Chill 5 minutes.

4. Remove a few cake pops at a time, and dip into melted candy to coat; gently tap off excess. Poke opposite ends of sticks into foam block. Immediately attach wings and two pieces of fondant for beak. Let stand until set. Spread two small dots of remaining 1 Tbsp. frosting onto head for eyes; top each with 1 black confetti candy and two black jimmies for lashes.

dainty daisy
cake pops

MAKES 54 CAKE POPS   Hands-On Time: 1 hour   Total Time: 3 hours

Gather up a bouquet of these posy pops for a birthday party, baby shower, or a weekend get-together of any kind!

1 (18.25-oz.) package party rainbow chip cake mix

Water, vegetable oil, and eggs called for on cake mix box

Wax paper

1 cup whipped ready-to-spread cream cheese frosting

2 cups pink candy melts

2 Tbsp. shortening

2 cups purple candy melts

54 paper lollipop sticks

Block of plastic foam

1 cup white candy melts, melted

54 yellow and orange candy-coated chocolate pieces

1. Preheat oven to 350°. Prepare and bake cake mix according to package directions for 13- x 9-inch pan, using water, oil, and eggs. Cool completely.

2. Line a baking sheet with wax paper. Crumble cake into large bowl. Add frosting; mix well. Shape into 54 (¼-inch) balls; place on baking sheet. Freeze until firm; transfer to refrigerator.

3. In a medium-sized microwave-safe bowl, heat pink candy melts and 1 Tbsp. shortening, uncovered, at MEDIUM (50% power) 1 minute, then in 15-second intervals until melted; stir until smooth. Repeat with purple candy melts and remaining 1 Tbsp. shortening. Dip tip of 1 lollipop stick about ½ inch into melted candy, and insert stick into 1 cake ball no more than halfway. Repeat with remaining sticks and cake balls. Return to baking sheet. Chill 5 minutes. Remove from refrigerator a few at a time. Dip half of cake balls into pink candy and half into purple candy; gently tap off excess. Poke opposite ends of sticks into foam block. Let stand until set.

4. Place melted white candy in a zip-top bag; snip off corner of bag. Pipe daisy petals on top of each cake pop. Place 1 chocolate candy in center of each. Let stand until set.

flower power
cookie pops

2 (17.5-oz.) pouches sugar cookie mix
¼ cup all-purpose flour
1 cup butter, softened
2 large eggs
¼ tsp. each red, yellow, green, blue,
     and purple food coloring paste
25 paper lollipop sticks

1. Preheat oven to 375°. In medium bowl, stir cookie mix, flour, butter, and eggs until dough forms. Divide dough evenly into 5 portions; tint each portion with different food coloring, kneading until blended.

2. Break off 2-inch portions of each color dough. On lightly floured surface, gently press dough portions together to form a large round, about 1 inch thick. Roll dough to ¼-inch thickness. Cut with 3-inch flower-shaped cookie cutter. Place cookies 2 inches apart on ungreased baking sheets. Insert 1 lollipop stick halfway into center of each cookie.

3. Bake at 375° for 10 to 12 minutes or until cookies are set. Cool 5 minutes; remove from baking sheets to wire racks. Cool completely.

color wow!

Turn these bold cookie pops into sweet, pastel-colored cookie pops by using only a drop or two of each food coloring.

patriotic cookie pops

MAKES 26 COOKIE POPS   Hands-On Time: 40 min.   Total Time: 4 hours

2 (17.5-oz.) pouches sugar cookie mix

½ cup all-purpose flour

1 cup butter, softened

2 large eggs

1 tsp. red food coloring paste

1 tsp. blue food coloring paste

2 tsp. white liquid food coloring

Cooking spray

26 paper lollipop sticks

1. In large bowl, stir cookie mix, flour, butter, and eggs until soft dough forms. Divide dough into thirds. Tint one-third of dough with red food coloring, kneading until completely blended. Repeat with another one-third of dough and blue food coloring. Tint remaining one-third of dough with white food coloring. Wrap each portion of dough in plastic wrap; chill 2 hours.

2. Preheat oven to 350°. Coat 2 baking sheets with cooking spray. Roll each color of dough into 26 (¾-inch) balls. Shape each ball into 12-inch rope. Place 1 each of red, blue, and white ropes together. Starting at 1 end, coil ropes to make a 2¾-inch-round cookie. Place 3 inches apart on baking sheets. Insert 1 lollipop stick into bottom of each cookie; chill 10 minutes.

3. Bake at 350° for 8 to 10 minutes or until bottoms are lightly golden. Cool 5 minutes; remove to wire racks. Cool completely (about 30 minutes).

simply smart

To ensure that color ropes stay distinct, chill cookies for 10 minutes before baking. Practice makes perfect when it comes to these pinwheels!

handpicked flower cookie pops

MAKES 14 COOKIE POPS Hands-On Time: 55 min. Total Time: 2 hours

1 (10.25-oz.) pouch fudge brownie mix

Water, vegetable oil, and eggs called for on brownie mix package

1 (17.5-oz.) pouch sugar cookie mix

½ cup butter, softened

1 large egg

¼ cup all-purpose flour

14 green craft sticks

6 oz. chocolate candy coating, melted

1 (16-oz.) container ready-to-spread cream cheese frosting

Orange, pink, and yellow food coloring paste

⅓ cup ready-to-spread chocolate frosting

1. Preheat oven to 350°. Prepare and bake brownies according to package directions for 8-inch square pan, using water, oil, and eggs. Cool completely. Scoop brownies by tablespoonfuls; roll into ¾-inch balls. Place 1 wooden pick halfway into each brownie ball. Chill 30 minutes. Increase oven temperature to 375°.

2. In medium bowl, stir cookie mix, butter, 1 egg, and flour with spoon until dough forms. On lightly floured surface, roll dough to ¼-inch thickness. Cut with 4-inch flower-shaped cookie cutter. Place 2 inches apart on ungreased baking sheet. Insert 1 craft stick into each cookie about halfway. Bake at 375° for 9 to 11 minutes. Remove from baking sheet to wire rack; cool completely (about 30 minutes).

3. Dip brownie balls into melted candy. Place in centers of flower cookies. Remove wooden picks. Let stand until set. Remove foil cover from cream cheese frosting; microwave at HIGH 20 seconds or until melted. Divide frosting among 3 bowls; tint 1 portion orange, 1 pink, and 1 yellow; spread on cookies. Place chocolate frosting in a zip-top plastic bag; snip off corner of bag. Pipe chocolate frosting in desired designs on cookies.

color wow!

For a bigger punch of color, sprinkle cookies with brightly colored sanding sugar immediately after frosting.

princess push-it-up cake pops

MAKES 12 PUSH-IT-UP POPS AND 48 MINI CUPCAKES

Hands-On Time: 35 min.   Total Time: 1 hour, 15 min.

Pretty as a princess, these pink and purple pops are like having 2 mini cupcakes in one!

Cooking spray

1 (18.25-oz.) package white cake mix

⅓ cup vegetable oil

3 large egg whites

Pink food coloring paste

2 (12-oz.) containers whipped ready-to-spread white frosting

Purple food coloring paste

Large disposable decorating bag

12 plastic push-it-up pop containers

1. Preheat oven to 350°. Coat 3 (24-cup) miniature muffin pans with cooking spray. In large bowl, beat cake mix, oil, egg whites, and 1¼ cups water at low speed with an electric mixer 30 seconds. Beat at high speed 2 minutes. Tint batter with pink food coloring, beating until blended. Divide batter among muffin cups, filling three-fourths full. Bake at 350° for 10 to 12 minutes or until a wooden pick inserted in center comes out clean. Cool 5 minutes; remove from pans to wire racks. Cool completely.

2. Divide frosting into 3 bowls. Tint 1 bowl of frosting purple. Tint 1 bowl of frosting pink. Leave remaining frosting white. Insert a large star tip into a large disposable decorating bag; place spoonfuls of each color frosting side by side, alternating colors and working up from tip of bag. Do not mix colors.

3. To assemble, drop 1 cupcake into each push-it-up pop container. Pipe frosting on cupcake. Top each with second cupcake; pipe frosting on cupcake. Frost remaining 48 cupcakes. Serve with push-it-up cakes, or freeze unfrosted cupcakes for later use.

Resource Note: Purchase push-it-up pop containers at www.amazon.com.

creamy orange push-it-up cake pops

MAKES 10 PUSH-IT-UP POPS   Hands-On Time: 26 min.   Total Time: 31 min.

If you love a frozen orange ice cream pop, then you're going to love our push pops!

1 (16-oz.) loaf frozen pound cake, thawed
1 (3.4-oz.) package vanilla instant pudding mix
1 cup milk
½ cup sour cream
Neon orange food coloring paste
1 tsp. orange zest, divided
3 disposable decorating bags
⅓ cup butter, softened
1½ cups powdered sugar
½ cup orange juice, divided
10 plastic push-it-up pop containers
Orange jimmies

1. Trim all edges from pound cake. Cut into 15 (½-inch-thick) slices. Cut each slice into 2 rounds using a 1¾-inch round cutter.

2. Whisk together pudding mix and milk until blended. Let stand until just thickened, about 5 minutes. Whisk in sour cream until blended. Transfer half of pudding mixture (¾ cup) to another bowl; stir in ⅛ tsp. neon orange food coloring paste and ½ tsp. orange zest to one bowl. Spoon pudding mixtures into each of 2 disposable decorating bags; cut off ½ inch from tip.

3. Beat butter at medium speed with an electric mixer until creamy. Add powdered sugar, 2 Tbsp. orange juice, and remaining ½ tsp. orange zest; beat at medium speed until well blended. Tint half of frosting orange. Insert a star tip into a disposable decorating bag; spoon orange frosting into one side of bag, and fill other side with plain frosting.

4. Place 1 pound cake round in bottom of each of 10 push-it-up pop containers. Spoon about ½ tsp. orange juice over pound cake. Pipe orange pudding on top. Repeat layers with 10 more pound cake rounds, orange juice, and vanilla pudding. Top with remaining pound cake rounds; drizzle with remaining orange juice. Pipe frosting on top; sprinkle with jimmies.

Resource Note: Purchase push-it-up pop containers at www.amazon.com.

meringue pops

MAKES 48 MERINGUE POPS   Hands-On Time: 21 min.   Total Time: 10 hours, 51 min.

These lighter-than-air lollipops would make for a sweet gift. Use any colors you like, or try piling up two to three colors in one pop!

4 large egg whites, at room
    temperature
½ tsp. cream of tartar
1 cup sugar
Yellow, pink, and green food coloring
    pastes
Disposable decorating bags
Parchment paper
48 paper lollipop sticks

1. Preheat oven to 200°. Beat egg whites at high speed with an electric mixer until foamy; add cream of tartar, beating until blended. Gradually add sugar, beating until stiff peaks form and sugar dissolves. Divide mixture evenly between 3 bowls (about 1½ cups per bowl).

2. Add ⅛ tsp. yellow food coloring paste to 1 bowl, gently folding until blended. Insert a large star tip into a decorating bag; spoon yellow meringue into bag. Pipe mixture into 16 (2-inch) rounds onto a parchment paper-lined baking sheet.

3. Add ⅛ tsp. pink food coloring paste to another bowl, gently folding until blended. Insert a large star tip into a decorating bag; spoon pink meringue into bag. Pipe mixture into 16 (2-inch) rounds onto a parchment paper-lined baking sheet.

4. Add ⅛ tsp. green food coloring paste to remaining bowl, gently folding until blended. Insert a large star tip into a decorating bag; spoon green meringue into bag. Pipe mixture into 16 (2-inch) rounds onto a parchment paper-lined baking sheet.

5. Bake at 200° for 2 hours. Turn off oven and let meringues stand in oven with light on for 8 hours. Carefully insert lollipop sticks halfway into each meringue.

chocolate-dipped cherry marshmallows

MAKES 16 POPS Hands-On Time: 42 min.   Total Time: 9 hours, 37 min.

½ cup cornstarch

½ cup powdered sugar

1 cup cold water, divided

1 (3-oz.) package cherry-flavored gelatin

1 (¼-oz.) envelope unflavored gelatin

1¾ cups granulated sugar

⅔ cup light corn syrup

½ tsp. vanilla extract

½ tsp. almond extract

16 chocolate-and-hazelnut-filled rolled wafers

⅓ cup pink candy melts, melted

6 oz. bittersweet chocolate, melted

Wax paper

pink piping

Spoon 2 Tbsp. melted pink candy melts into a small zip-top freezer bag. Snip 1 corner of bag to make a small hole. Pipe melted candy on sides of chocolate-covered marshmallows; let stand 10 minutes, or until set.

1. Line bottom and sides of a 13- x 9-inch pan with lightly greased aluminum foil. Whisk together cornstarch and powdered sugar in a small bowl. Dust ⅓ cup cornstarch mixture onto prepared pan.

2. Pour ½ cup water in bowl of a heavy-duty electric stand mixer. Sprinkle cherry and plain gelatin over cold water; stir and let stand 5 minutes.

3. Stir together remaining ½ cup water, granulated sugar, and corn syrup in medium saucepan over medium-high heat, and cook until a candy thermometer measures 240°, about 11 minutes.

4. Beat gelatin mixture at low speed of electric stand mixer using whisk attachment, and pour in hot syrup. Increase speed to medium-high, and beat 8 to 10 minutes or until very thick and just slightly warm. Add extracts; beat until blended. Spoon mixture into prepared pan, and smooth top with a lightly greased offset spatula. Dust with ⅓ cup cornstarch mixture, cover, and let stand at room temperature 8 hours or until firm.

5. Lift marshmallow mixture from pan, using foil as handles. Gently remove foil. Cut into 16 squares using a serrated knife. Dust marshmallow squares with remaining cornstarch mixture. Dip ½ inch of each rolled wafer into melted pink candy, and insert wafer halfway into marshmallow squares. Dip top ⅓ of each marshmallow into melted chocolate, and place on a waxed paper-lined baking sheet. Let stand 45 minutes or until chocolate has set.

mini glazed doughnuts on a stick

MAKES 46 DOUGHNUT POPS   Hands-On Time: 25 min.   Total Time: 1 hour, 55 min.

1 (15.25-oz.) package yellow cake mix

½ cup buttermilk

2 Tbsp. unsalted butter, melted

3 large eggs

1½ cups cake flour

½ tsp. ground cinnamon

Vegetable oil

2½ cups powdered sugar

¼ cup milk

½ tsp. vanilla extract

Dash pink food coloring gel

½ cup rainbow candy sprinkles

46 lollipop sticks

1. Beat cake mix, buttermilk, melted butter, eggs, cake flour, and cinnamon by hand with a wooden spoon until blended. Chill dough until firm (about 1 hour).

2. Place dough on a lightly floured surface, and roll to ½-inch thickness. Cut with a 1½-inch round cutter, flouring the cutter frequently. Cut a circle out of center of each doughnut with a ¾-inch round cutter.

3. Pour oil to depth of 2 inches into a Dutch oven; heat over medium heat to 365°. Fry doughnuts, in batches, about 30 seconds on each side or until golden brown. Drain on paper towels, and cool completely before glazing.

4. Whisk together powdered sugar, milk, and vanilla until smooth, adding additional milk, if necessary, for desired consistency. Stir in pink food coloring gel until well blended. Dip 1 side of each doughnut in glaze; top with sprinkles. Insert a lollipop stick into 1 end of each doughnut. Let stand 30 minutes or until glaze is set.

simply smart

Use the bottom of a piping tip as a ¾-inch cutter, or look for small fondant cutters to cut out the mini doughnut centers.

key lime pie pops

MAKES 18 PIE POPS   Hands-On Time: 30 min.   Total Time: 4 hours, 45 min.

Cool down with one of these tangy pie pops. Keep a few in the freezer for a fun treat when the weather's warm.

1 (14-oz.) can sweetened condensed milk

1 tsp. lime zest

½ cup bottled or fresh Key lime or regular lime juice

3 large egg yolks

10 drops yellow liquid food coloring

8 drops green liquid food coloring

9 single-serve graham cracker crusts (from 2 [4-oz.] packages)

Wax paper

18 craft sticks

12 oz. almond bark candy coating

1. Preheat oven to 375°. In medium bowl, whisk together condensed milk, lime zest, lime juice, egg yolks, and food colorings. Pour into crusts. Place on baking sheet. Bake at 375° for 10 to 12 minutes or until centers are set. Cool 15 minutes. Cover and chill at least 2 hours. Freeze until firm, about 30 minutes.

2. Line baking sheet with wax paper. Carefully remove frozen pies from pans; cut in half. Place pies on baking sheet. Pierce side of each pie with a knife; insert craft stick into side of each pie through crust and about 1½ inches into filling. Freeze 1 hour or until very firm.

3. In small microwave-safe bowl, heat candy coating at HIGH 1 to 2 minutes, stirring every 30 seconds until smooth. Remove 3 or 4 pie pops from freezer at a time. Dip bottom crust and cut sides of pie pops into melted coating; gently tap off excess. Return dipped pops to baking sheet. Freeze until firm, about 15 minutes. Spoon remaining melted coating into small zip-top plastic bag. Cut off 1 tiny corner of bag. Squeeze bag to pipe coating onto pies to look like lime slices. Keep pops frozen.

green with envy candy apples

MAKES 12 CANDY APPLES Hands-On Time: 26 min. Total Time: 1 hour, 36 min.

The combination of a sweet hard candy shell on the outside and tart apple on the inside is always a favorite. We've traded the traditional red candy for Kelly green to go along with the Granny Smiths.

12 small Granny Smith apples

12 craft sticks or candy sticks

2½ cups sugar

½ cup light corn syrup

⅛ tsp. Kelly green food coloring
    paste

Parchment paper

1. Remove stems from apples, and insert craft sticks.

2. Combine sugar, corn syrup, and ⅔ cup water in a heavy 2-qt. saucepan. Bring to a boil over medium heat, stirring occasionally. Boil 13 minutes, without stirring, until a candy thermometer registers 300° (hard crack stage). Immediately remove from heat; stir in food coloring.

3. Dip each apple in syrup, tilting pan and turning apples to coat evenly; allow excess syrup to drip off. Place apples on a parchment paper-lined baking sheet. Let stand until set, about 10 minutes.

color wow!

Decorate candy apples with colorful gummy worms for a playful look. Cellophane bags and colorful ribbons turn them into perfect party favors.

crazy for
cupcakes

banana split cupcakes

MAKES 48 CUPCAKES   Hands-On Time: 25 min.   Total Time: 1 hour, 45 min.

Get away with having 3 cupcakes for dessert with our play on a banana split—don't worry, they're minis!

Miniature paper baking cups

1 (18.25-oz.) package yellow cake mix

1 cup mashed very ripe bananas (2 medium)

½ cup vegetable oil

3 large eggs

1 (16-oz.) container ready-to-spread chocolate frosting

Large disposable decorating bag

1 (16-oz.) container ready-to-spread vanilla or creamy white frosting

1 (12-oz.) container whipped ready-to-spread strawberry frosting

48 maraschino cherries with stems, patted dry

¼ cup rainbow candy sprinkles

1. Preheat oven to 350°. Place a mini paper baking cup in each of 24 mini muffin cups. In large bowl, beat cake mix, bananas, oil, ¼ cup water, and eggs at low speed with an electric mixer 30 seconds. Beat at medium speed 2 minutes. Spoon batter into cups, filling two-thirds full. (Cover and refrigerate remaining batter until ready to bake.)

2. Bake at 350° for 12 to 15 minutes or until a wooden pick inserted in center comes out clean. Cool in pan on wire racks 5 minutes; remove from pans to wire racks. Cool completely (about 30 minutes). Repeat with remaining batter to make 24 more mini cupcakes.

3. In small microwave-safe bowl, reserve ¼ cup of the chocolate frosting. Insert a large star tip into a large decorating bag; fill with remaining cholocate frosting. Pipe frosting onto 16 cupcakes. Repeat with white and strawberry frosting. Microwave reserved chocolate frosting on HIGH 20 to 25 seconds or until smooth. Cool 1 minute; drizzle over frosting on each cupcake. Pipe a dab of white frosting on each; top each with a cherry and sprinkles.

flowerpot cupcakes

MAKES 24 CUPCAKES   Hands-On Time: 50 min.   Total Time: 1 hour, 30 min.

Parchment paper
1 (16-oz.) package ready-to-bake
    refrigerated sugar cookies
    (not roll)
¼ cup all-purpose flour, divided
24 green wooden picks
¼ tsp. orange food coloring paste
¼ tsp. brown food coloring paste
Shortening
¾ cup devil's food cake mix
2 Tbsp. vegetable oil
1 large egg
½ cup ready-to-spread chocolate
    frosting
4 thin chocolate wafer cookies,
    crushed
1 cup powdered sugar
Purple food coloring paste
Yellow food coloring paste
12 spearmint gumdrops

1. Preheat oven to 350°. Line a baking sheet with parchment paper. Remove 8 squares of cookie dough from package; refrigerate remaining dough until needed. Sprinkle 2 Tbsp. flour onto work surface. On floured surface, roll dough to ⅛-inch thickness. Cut 24 cookies using 1½-inch flower-shaped cookie cutter. Place about 2 inches apart on prepared baking sheet. Insert a wooden pick halfway into each cookie. Bake at 350° for 8 to 10 minutes or until light golden brown.

2. Remove remaining dough from package; mix orange and brown food coloring into dough until color is evenly blended. Sprinkle remaining 2 Tbsp. flour onto work surface. On floured surface, roll orange dough to ⅛-inch thickness. Cut 24 cookies using 2¼-inch round cutter. Grease 24 miniature muffin cups with shortening. Press dough rounds in bottoms and up sides of miniature muffin cups; refrigerate 15 minutes.

3. In medium bowl, beat cake mix, 3 Tbsp. water, oil, and egg with a whisk until blended; fill muffin cups halfway. Bake at 350° for 18 to 22 minutes or until a wooden pick inserted in center comes out clean. Cool completely in pan. Remove from pan. Frost cupcakes with chocolate frosting, and sprinkle with cookie crumbs.

4. In small bowl, mix powdered sugar and 1 Tbsp. water until smooth; divide into 2 bowls. Tint glazes purple and yellow; spread on flower cookies. Dot center of flower cookies with other color. Insert flower cookies into cupcakes. Flatten each gumdrop; cut each into 4 leaf shapes. Place 2 leaves at base of each flower.

shark frenzy cupcakes

MAKES 24 CUPCAKES   Hands-On Time: 21 min.   Total Time: 1 hour, 14 min.

Blue paper baking cups

1 (16.25-oz.) package white cake mix

Water, vegetable oil, and egg whites called for on cake mix box

Royal blue food coloring paste

1 cup butter, softened

4 cups powdered sugar

1 tsp. vanilla extract

½ tsp. almond extract

3 large disposable decorating bags

Shark-shaped chewy candies

1. Preheat oven to 350°. Place paper baking cups in 2 (12-cup) muffin pans. Prepare cake mix according to package directions for cupcakes, using water, oil, and egg whites; tint batter light blue, using desired amount of food coloring. Spoon batter into cups, filling two-thirds full.

2. Bake at 350° for 18 minutes or until a wooden pick inserted in center comes out clean. Cool in pans on wire racks 5 minutes; remove from pans to wire racks, and cool completely (about 30 minutes).

3. Beat butter at medium speed with an electric mixer until creamy; gradually add powdered sugar, beating well. Beat in vanilla and almond extracts. Divide frosting between 2 bowls. Tint one bowl with a dash of royal blue food coloring paste. Tint second bowl with ¼ tsp. royal blue food coloring paste. Spoon frosting into each of 2 decorating bags. Snip off the ends, and set both bags into another large decorating bag fitted with a large star tip. Pipe frosting onto cupcakes; top with shark candies.

color wow!

Before frosting cupcakes, place close together on a serving platter. Frost cupcake tops to look like a continuous sea of blue waves.

blackberry-citrus cupcakes

MAKES 24 CUPCAKES   Hands-On Time: 35 min.   Total Time: 1 hour, 35 min.

Fresh blackberry juice in the frosting marries beautifully with the lemony zing in the cupcakes. Pile on the frosting, fresh berries, and mint leaves for a dramatic look.

Paper baking cups
1 (18.25-oz.) package lemon cake mix
Water, vegetable oil, and eggs called
　　for on cake mix box
1 Tbsp. lemon zest
1 cup fresh blackberries
1½ cups butter, softened
3 cups powdered sugar
Garnishes: fresh blackberries, fresh
　　mint leaves

1. Preheat oven to 350°. Place paper baking cups in 2 (12-cup) muffin pans.

2. Prepare cake mix according to package directions for cupcakes, using water, oil, and eggs and adding lemon zest. Spoon batter into cups, filling two-thirds full. Bake at 350° for 18 minutes or until a wooden pick inserted in center comes out clean. Cool in pans on wire racks 10 minutes; remove from pans to wire racks. Cool completely (about 30 minutes).

3. Place 1 cup blackberries in a small microwave-safe bowl. Cover; microwave at HIGH 60 seconds to 90 seconds, stirring once, until softened. Mash with fork. Place fine, wire-mesh strainer over clean small bowl; line strainer with cheesecloth. Pour berries into strainer; press with back of spoon to remove seeds. Reserve juice; discard seeds and pulp.

4. In large bowl, beat butter and powdered sugar at low speed with an electric mixer until blended. Gradually add reserved blackberry juice, beating at high speed until frosting is smooth and spreadable. Frost cupcakes.

tie-dyed cupcakes

MAKES 24 CUPCAKES   Hands-On Time: 45 min.   Total Time: 2 hours, 45 min.

We chose hot pink, green, and turquoise for our tie-dyed color palette, but just about any color combination will make for some totally rad cupcakes!

White paper baking cups

1 (18.25-oz.) package white cake mix

Water, vegetable oil, and egg whites called for on cake mix box

Hot pink food coloring paste

Green food coloring paste

Turquoise food coloring paste

1 cup butter, softened

2 (16-oz.) packages powdered sugar

2/3 cup milk

1 Tbsp. vanilla extract

Large 16-inch disposable decorating bag

1. Preheat oven to 350°. Place white paper baking cups in 2 (12-cup) muffin pans. Prepare cake mix according to package directions for cupcakes, using water, oil, and egg whites. Divide batter evenly among 3 medium bowls. Add a different food coloring to each bowl to make hot pink, green, and turquoise. Place 1 level Tbsp. of each color batter into each muffin cup, layering colors (do not stir). Each cup will be about one-half full. Bake at 350° for 17 to 23 minutes or until a wooden pick inserted in center comes out clean. Cool in pans on wire racks 10 minutes. Remove to wire racks. Cool completely (about 30 minutes).

2. Beat butter at medium speed with an electric mixer until creamy; gradually add powdered sugar alternately with milk, beating at low speed until blended after each addition. Stir in vanilla extract.

3. Divide frosting evenly among 3 medium bowls. Tint 1 hot pink, 1 green, and 1 turquoise with food coloring. Refrigerate about 30 minutes. Insert a star tip in a large decorating bag; place spoonfuls of each color frosting side by side in bag, alternating colors and working up from tip of bag. Do not stir colors together. Starting at twelve o'clock on outer edge of each cupcake and using constant pressure on bag, pipe frosting clockwise for 3 rotations, working toward center and ending in small peak.

pound cake cupcakes

MAKES 30 CUPCAKES   Hands-On Time: 30 min.   Total Time: 2 hours, 5 min.

Paper baking cups
1 cup butter, softened
2½ cups sugar
6 large eggs
3 cups all-purpose flour
1 tsp. baking powder
1 (8-oz.) container mascarpone
    cheese, softened
3 tsp. vanilla extract, divided
9 (2-oz.) vanilla candy coating
    squares, coarsely chopped
½ cup whipping cream
2 Tbsp. butter, softened
Sky blue food coloring paste
Candy flowers

1. Preheat oven to 350°. Place 30 paper baking cups in 3 (12-cup) muffin pans. Beat 1 cup butter at medium speed with an electric mixer until fluffy; gradually add sugar, beating well. Add eggs, 1 at a time, beating just until blended after each addition.

2. Stir together flour and baking powder. Add flour mixture to butter mixture alternately with mascarpone cheese, beginning and ending with flour mixture. Beat at low speed just until blended after each addition. Stir in 2 tsp. vanilla. Spoon batter into cups using a 4 Tbsp. (¼-cup) cookie scoop.

3. Bake at 350° for 20 to 23 minutes or until a wooden pick inserted in center comes out clean. Cool in pans on wire racks 10 minutes. Remove to wire racks. Cool completely (about 30 minutes).

4. Microwave vanilla candy coating and whipping cream in a 1-qt. microwave-safe bowl at MEDIUM (50% power) 1½ minutes. Stir mixture, and microwave 1 more minute or until candy coating is almost melted, gently stirring at 30-second intervals. Whisk until melted and smooth. (Do not overheat or overwhisk.) Whisk in 2 Tbsp. softened butter and remaining 1 tsp. vanilla. Tint with desired amount of food coloring paste.

5. Working quickly, dip tops of cupcakes in candy mixture. Place right side up on a wire rack. (If mixture begins to harden, microwave 10 to 15 seconds, and stir until smooth.) Top with candy flowers.

Resource Note: Look for candy flowers in baking aisle.

sundae cupcakes

MAKES 24 CUPCAKES   Hands-On Time: 45 min.   Total Time: 1 hour, 45 min.

Paper baking cups
1 cup Dutch process cocoa
2 cups boiling water
1 cup butter, softened
2 cups sugar
4 large eggs
2½ cups all-purpose flour
1 tsp. baking soda
1 tsp. baking powder
½ tsp. table salt
1 tsp. vanilla extract
Large disposable decorating bag
2 (16-oz.) containers ready-to-spread
    vanilla or creamy white frosting
Rainbow candy sprinkles or
    multicolored jimmies
1 cup hot fudge topping
24 red maraschino cherries with
    stems
6 waffle cones, broken into large
    pieces

1. Preheat oven to 350°. Place paper baking cups in 2 (12-cup) muffin pans. Whisk together cocoa and 2 cups boiling water in a large heatproof bowl. Cool completely (about 10 minutes).

2. Beat butter at medium speed with an electric mixer until creamy; gradually add sugar, beating until blended. Add eggs, 1 at a time, beating just until blended after each addition.

3. Stir together flour and next 3 ingredients; add to butter mixture alternately with cocoa mixture, beginning and ending with flour mixture. Beat at low speed just until blended after each addition. Stir in vanilla. Spoon batter into cups, filling three-fourths full.

4. Bake at 350° for 18 to 20 minutes or until a wooden pick inserted in center comes out clean. Cool in pans on wire racks 10 minutes; remove from pans to wire racks, and cool completely (about 30 minutes).

5. Insert a large star tip into a large decorating bag; fill with vanilla frosting. Pipe frosting onto cupcakes. Roll edges of frosted cupcakes in sprinkles.

6. Microwave hot fudge topping in a small glass bowl at HIGH 5 to 15 seconds or until barely warm and fluid; spoon over frosting, letting drip down sides. Top each cupcake with a cherry. Insert a piece of waffle cone into side of frosting.

margarita cupcakes

MAKES 24 CUPCAKES   Hands-On Time: 1 hour   Total Time: 2 hours, 5 min.

Paper baking cups
1 (18.25-oz.) package lemon cake mix
½ cup vegetable oil
½ cup gold tequila or water
1 tsp. orange zest
3 large eggs
1 (3-oz.) package lime-flavored
  gelatin
2 (12-oz.) containers whipped ready-
  to-spread white frosting
1 tsp. electric green food coloring gel
¼ cup coarse white sugar or white
  decorator sugar crystals
24 thin lime slices (about 3 limes)
24 cocktail umbrellas (optional)

1. Preheat oven to 350°. Place paper baking cups in 2 (12-cup) muffin pans.

2. In large bowl, beat cake mix, next 5 ingredients, and ½ cup water at low speed with an electric mixer 30 seconds. Beat at medium speed 2 minutes, scraping bowl occasionally. Spoon batter evenly into muffin cups, filling two-thirds full.

3. Bake at 350° for 18 to 22 minutes or until a wooden pick inserted in center comes out clean. Cool in pans on wire racks 10 minutes; remove from pans to wire racks, and cool completely (about 30 minutes).

4. In medium bowl, mix frosting and food coloring until blended. Frost cupcakes. Sprinkle sugar on small plate; roll edges of cupcakes in sugar. Roll edges of lime slices in sugar; place on cupcakes. Poke 1 umbrella into each cupcake, if desired. Store loosely covered in refrigerator.

simply smart

The colorful cocktail umbrellas not only give these cupcakes a fun, beachy look, but when cupcakes are covered, they also keep plastic wrap from smearing the frosting.

pretty in pink
cupcakes

MAKES 12 CUPCAKES   Hands-On Time: 35 min.   Total Time: 1 hour, 45 min.

Jumbo paper baking cups
½ cup butter, softened
1 cup shortening
2 cups sugar
4 large eggs
2¾ cups all-purpose flour
2 tsp. baking powder
½ tsp. table salt
1 cup buttermilk
1½ tsp. vanilla extract
1½ tsp. almond extract
Pink food coloring paste
3 (12-oz.) containers whipped ready-
   to-spread white frosting
1 large disposable decorating bag
   (16-inch)
Garnish: edible light pink pearls

1. Preheat oven to 350°. Place paper baking cups in 2 (6-cup) jumbo muffin pans. Beat butter and shortening at medium speed with an electric mixer until creamy; gradually add sugar, beating well. Add eggs, 1 at a time, beating just until blended after each addition.

2. Stir together flour, baking powder, and salt; add to butter mixture alternately with buttermilk, beginning and ending with flour mixture. Beat at low speed just until blended after each addition. Stir in extracts.

3. Divide batter evenly among 4 bowls. Using the tip of a wooden pick, dip 1 end into food coloring paste, and then swipe coloring into 1 bowl; blend to make very pale pink. Color each bowl of remaining batter gradually darker shades of pink.

4. Starting with darkest pink batter, spoon batter evenly into cups. Repeat procedure with remaining colors of batter, ending with lightest shade of pink on top (do not stir). Each cup will be about three-fourths full.

5. Bake at 350° for 28 to 30 minutes or until a wooden pick inserted in center comes out clean. Cool in pans on wire racks 10 minutes; remove from pans to wire racks, and cool completely (about 30 minutes).

6. Divide frosting evenly among 2 medium bowls. Tint frostings light pink and dark pink. Insert a star tip into large decorating bag; spoon light pink frosting up one side of bag and dark pink frosting up other. Pipe frosting onto cupcakes in a spiral pattern.

red, white, and blue swirl cupcakes

MAKES 24 CUPCAKES   Hands-On Time: 30 min.   Total Time: 1 hour, 35 min.

Paper baking cups

1 (18.25-oz.) package white cake mix

Water, vegetable oil, and eggs called for on cake mix box

1 (1-oz.) bottle red liquid food coloring

2 cups butter, softened

1 (32-oz.) bag powdered sugar

½ to ¾ cup milk

1½ tsp. royal blue food coloring paste

Large disposable decorating bag

Edible gold star glitter

1. Preheat oven to 350°. Place paper baking cups in 2 (12-cup) muffin pans. Prepare and bake cake mix according to package directions for cupcakes, using water, oil, and eggs and adding red food coloring. Cool in pans on wire racks 10 minutes; remove from pans to wire racks. Cool completely (about 30 minutes).

2. In large bowl, beat butter and half the powdered sugar at medium speed with an electric mixer until smooth. Gradually add remaining powdered sugar alternately with milk, beating until frosting is smooth and spreadable. Divide frosting between 2 bowls. Stir desired amount blue food coloring into 1 bowl until blended.

3. Insert a star tip into large decorating bag. Place spoonfuls of white and blue frosting side by side, alternating colors and working up from tip of bag (do not stir). Starting at 12 o'clock on outer edge of each cupcake and using constant pressure on bag, pipe frosting clockwise for 3 rotations, working toward center and ending in small peak. Decorate with edible glitter. Store loosely covered.

color wow!

Choose festive red, white, and blue cupcake liners for an over-the-top look, or serve cupcakes in colorful small cups as pictured.

lemon-lavender cupcakes

MAKES 24 CUPCAKES   Hands-On Time: 30 min.   Total Time: 3 hours, 30 min.

Roses are red; violets are blue. Lavender is purple, and these cupcakes are, too! Plus, they are filled with a surprise lemon filling.

1 (2.9-oz.) package lemon cook-and-serve pudding mix
Paper baking cups
1 (16.25-oz.) package white cake mix
Water, vegetable oil, and egg whites called for on cake mix box
¼ cup milk
1 Tbsp. dried lavender
1¼ cups butter, softened
4 cups powdered sugar
Dash of violet food coloring paste
Garnish: lemon rind curls or sugared or fresh violas/pansies

1. Prepare lemon pudding according to package directions. Remove from heat; pour pudding into a bowl. Place heavy-duty plastic wrap directly on warm pudding (to prevent a film from forming); refrigerate until thoroughly chilled, about 3 hours.

2. Preheat oven to 350°. Place paper baking cups in 2 (12-cup) muffin pans. Prepare and bake cake mix according to package directions for cupcakes, using water, oil, and egg whites; bake as directed, and cool completely (about 30 minutes).

3. Cook milk in a small heavy nonaluminum saucepan over medium-low heat, stirring often, just until bubbles appear (do not boil); remove from heat. Stir in lavender; let stand 5 minutes. Pour mixture through a fine wire-mesh strainer; discard lavender. Cool completely (about 10 minutes).

4. Beat butter at medium-low speed with an electric mixer until creamy; gradually add powdered sugar, beating well. Add 3 Tbsp. milk mixture and food coloring; beat until fluffy. Set aside.

5. Cut cone shape out of top of cupcakes, about ¼ inch from the edge and ½ inch from the bottom using a small serrated knife. Fill each cupcake with 1 Tbsp. lemon pudding (reserve remaining pudding for another use); replace tops. Pipe frosting on tops of cupcakes.

watermelon cupcakes

MAKES 24 CUPCAKES   Hands-On Time: 30 min.   Total Time: 1 hour, 40 min.

Paper baking cups
1 (18.25-oz.) package vanilla cake mix
Water, vegetable oil, and eggs called
    for on cake mix box
½ tsp. green food coloring paste
1 cup butter, softened
1 (32-oz.) bag powdered sugar
3 Tbsp. watermelon-flavored gelatin
    (from 3-oz. box)
⅓ cup milk
1½ tsp. red food coloring paste
Large disposable decorating bag
¼ cup miniature semisweet chocolate
    morsels

1. Preheat oven to 350°. Place paper baking cups in 2 (12-cup) muffin pans.

2. Prepare cake mix according to package directions for cupcakes, using water, oil, and eggs and adding green food coloring. Cool in pans on wire racks 10 minutes; remove from pans to wire racks. Cool completely (about 30 minutes).

3. In large bowl, beat butter and half of powdered sugar at medium speed with an electric mixer until smooth. Beat in gelatin (dry) until blended. Gradually add remaining powdered sugar alternately with milk, beating until frosting is smooth and spreadable. Beat in red food coloring.

4. Insert a large star tip into decorating bag; fill with frosting. Pipe frosting onto cupcakes. Decorate with chocolate morsels to look like watermelon seeds.

color wow!

Tint frosting as dark or as pale as you like. If you're looking for knock-out-bright watermelon color, use electric pink and red food colorings together.

neapolitan cupcakes

MAKES 24 CUPCAKES   Hands-On Time: 35 min.   Total Time: 1 hour, 30 min.

These layered cupcakes are not only colored pink, white, and brown, but they are also flavored with strawberry, chocolate, and vanilla.

White paper baking cups
1 (18.25-oz.) package white cake mix
Water, vegetable oil, and eggs called for on cake mix box
½ tsp. almond extract
½ tsp. vanilla extract
¼ cup unsweetened cocoa
½ cup miniature semisweet chocolate morsels
1 (12-oz.) container whipped ready-to-spread chocolate frosting
1 (12-oz.) container whipped ready-to-spread fluffy white frosting
1 (12-oz.) container whipped ready-to-spread strawberry mist frosting
Pink and white jimmies
Additional miniature semisweet chocolate morsels

1. Preheat oven to 350°. Place white paper baking cups in 2 (12-cup) muffin pans.

2. Prepare cake mix according to package directions for cupcakes, using water, oil, and eggs and adding almond and vanilla extracts. Pour half of batter into a small bowl; stir in cocoa and ½ cup chocolate morsels. Divide chocolate batter evenly among muffin cups. Carefully spoon white batter evenly over chocolate batter.

3. Bake at 350° according to package directions. Cool in pans on wire racks 10 minutes. Remove from pans to wire racks, and cool completely (about 30 minutes).

4. Frost cupcakes with a layer each of chocolate frosting, white frosting, and strawberry frosting. Decorate with jimmies and additional chocolate morsels.

lemon ombre cupcakes

MAKES 24 CUPCAKES   Hands-On Time: 35 min.   Total Time: 1 hour, 28 min.

Paper baking cups
1 (18.25-oz.) package French vanilla
    cake mix
Water, vegetable oil, and eggs called
    for on cake mix box
2 Tbsp. lemon zest
Golden yellow food coloring paste
Lemon yellow food coloring paste
1½ cups butter, softened
6 cups powdered sugar
½ cup lemon curd

1. Preheat oven to 350°. Place paper baking cups in 2 (12-cup) muffin pans. Prepare cake mix according to package directions for cupcakes, using water, oil, and eggs; stir in lemon zest.

2. Combine 2¾ cups batter and ¼ tsp. golden yellow food coloring in a small bowl. Spoon batter evenly into 12 muffin cups. Combine 1¾ cups batter and ¼ tsp. lemon yellow food coloring in a separate small bowl. Spoon batter evenly into 8 muffin cups. Combine remaining 1 cup batter with a dash of lemon yellow color in a separate bowl. Spoon batter evenly into remaining 4 muffin cups.

3. Bake at 350° for 18 minutes or until a wooden pick inserted in center comes out clean. Cool in pans on wire racks 5 minutes. Remove from pans to wire racks, and cool completely (about 30 minutes).

4. Beat butter at medium speed with an electric mixer until creamy; gradually add powdered sugar, beating well. Add lemon curd, beating until fluffy, about 3 minutes.

5. Tint 2¾ cups frosting with ¼ tsp. golden yellow food coloring in a medium bowl. Pipe or spread frosting evenly onto 12 darkest-colored cupcakes. Tint 1½ cups frosting with ¼ tsp. lemon yellow food coloring in a separate bowl. Pipe or spread frosting evenly onto 8 medium-colored cupcakes. Tint remaining ¾ cup frosting with a dash of lemon yellow food coloring in a separate bowl. Pipe or spread frosting onto 4 lightest-colored cupcakes. Arrange cupcakes on a tiered cake stand.

rockin' purple cupcakes

MAKES 24 CUPCAKES   Hands-On Time: 35 min.   Total Time: 1 hour, 30 min.

Colorful rock candy can take a simple cupcake from "Mmm" to "Wow!" Choose solid or multicolor candy, and pile it on.

Paper baking cups

1 (15.25-oz.) package chocolate fudge cake mix with pudding

Water, vegetable oil, and eggs called for on cake mix box

2 (12-oz.) containers whipped ready-to-spread white frosting

½ tsp. purple food coloring paste

2 Tbsp. black sanding sugar

½ cup purple rock candy

1. Preheat oven to 350°. Place paper baking cups in 2 (12-cup) muffin pans. Prepare and bake cake mix according to package directions for cupcakes, using water, oil, and eggs. Cool in pans on wire racks 10 minutes; remove from pans to wire racks. Cool completely (about 30 minutes).

2. Spoon frosting into medium bowl; tint with purple food coloring to desired color. Frost cupcakes. Sprinkle with sanding sugar. Top with rock candy.

Resource Note: You can buy rock candy online at www.ohnuts.com.

may flowers cupcakes

MAKES 24 CUPCAKES   Hands-On Time: 35 min.   Total Time: 1 hour, 30 min.

Paper baking cups
1 (18.25-oz.) package white cake mix
Water, vegetable oil, and egg whites
   called for on cake mix box
1 (3-oz.) package raspberry-flavored
   gelatin
2 (12-oz.) containers whipped ready-
   to-spread cream cheese frosting
24 large marshmallows
Assorted sanding sugars
24 small yellow gumdrops

1. Preheat oven to 350°. Place paper baking cups in 2 (12-cup) muffin pans.

2. Prepare cake mix according to package directions for cupcakes, using water, oil, and egg whites and adding gelatin. Spoon batter evenly into muffin cups, filling two-thirds full.

3. Bake at 350° for 18 to 22 minutes or until a wooden pick inserted in center comes out clean. Cool in pans on wire racks 10 minutes; remove from pans to wire racks. Cool completely (about 30 minutes).

4. Frost cupcakes with frosting. With dampened kitchen scissors, cut each marshmallow into 5 slices. Arrange slices on cupcakes in flower shape; sprinkle with sanding sugar. Use frosting to attach 1 gumdrop in center of each flower.

color wow!

Use a variety of colored sanding sugars to get a platter of multicolored flower cupcakes. Tie long, colorful ribbons around base of cupcakes for a festive May Day look!

brilliant dahlia cupcakes

MAKES 24 CUPCAKES   Hands-On Time: 45 min.   Total Time: 1 hour, 45 min.

Paper baking cups

1 cup shortening

½ cup butter, softened

2 cups sugar

4 large eggs

2½ cups all-purpose flour

2 tsp. baking powder

¼ tsp. table salt

1 cup buttermilk

1½ tsp. almond extract

1½ tsp. vanilla extract

Brilliant Frosting

Rose, lemon yellow, and orange food
     coloring paste

3 disposable decorating bags

Edible black, yellow, and pink pearls

brilliant frosting

Beat 1 cup butter, 2 tsp. vanilla extract, and ¼ tsp. table salt at medium speed with an electric mixer until creamy. Gradually add 2 (16-oz.) packages powdered sugar alternately with ½ cup whipping cream, beating at low speed until blended after each addition. Beat at high speed 2 minutes or until creamy.

1. Preheat oven to 350°. Place paper baking cups in 2 (12-cup) muffin pans. Beat shortening and butter at medium speed with an electric mixer until creamy; gradually add sugar, beating until blended. Add eggs, 1 at a time, beating just until blended after each addition.

2. Stir together flour, baking powder, and salt; add to butter mixture alternately with buttermilk, beginning and ending with flour mixture. Beat at low speed just until blended after each addition. Stir in almond extract and vanilla extract. Spoon batter into muffin cups, filling two-thirds full.

3. Bake at 350° for 18 to 20 minutes or until a wooden pick inserted in center comes out clean. Cool in pans on wire racks 10 minutes; remove from pans to wire racks, and cool completely (about 30 minutes).

4. Divide Brilliant Frosting evenly into 3 bowls. Tint one bowl of frosting with rose food coloring paste. Tint the second bowl with lemon yellow food coloring paste. Tint the third bowl with orange food coloring paste. Spoon each color frosting into individual decorating bags fitted with a large leaf tip.

5. Working from center of cupcakes to edge, pipe pink frosting into petal shapes, layering petals around outside edges while leaving frosting in center flat for edible pearls.

6. Fill center of each cupcake with edible pearls. Repeat procedure with yellow and orange frosting.

Step 4

Step 5

Step 6

king cake cupcakes

MAKES 12 CUPCAKES   Hands-On Time: 14 min.   Total Time: 30 min.

These shortcut sweets make enjoying Mardi Gras easy, as each little cake can be eaten out of hand.

½ (8-oz.) package cream cheese, softened
¼ cup butter, softened
1½ cups powdered sugar
¼ tsp. vanilla extract
2 to 3 Tbsp. half-and-half
12 unfrosted, store-bought cupcakes
Green-, purple-, and gold-tinted sanding sugars

1. Beat cream cheese and butter at medium speed with an electric mixer until creamy. Gradually add sugar, beating until blended. Stir in vanilla and 2 Tbsp. half-and-half. Add remaining half-and-half, 1 tsp. at a time, until desired consistency.

2. Spread frosting over cupcakes, letting frosting run over edges. Sprinkle with sanding sugars, alternating colors and forming bands.

simply smart

If desired, insert a small plastic baby doll token into one cupcake before frosting. According to Mardi Gras tradition, the one who picks the special cupcake brings the king cake cupcakes next year!

swirled candy cane cupcakes

MAKES 24 CUPCAKES   Hands-On Time: 35 min.   Total Time: 1 hour, 30 min.

Paper baking cups

1 (18.25-oz.) package white cake mix

Water, vegetable oil, and egg whites called for on cake mix box

1 tsp. peppermint extract

1 tsp. red food coloring paste

2 (12-oz.) containers whipped ready-to-spread white frosting

1 cup crushed hard peppermint candies (about 30)

1. Preheat oven to 350°. Place paper baking cups in 2 (12-cup) muffin pans.

2. Prepare cake mix according to package directions for cupcakes, using water, oil, and egg whites and adding peppermint extract. Divide batter in half. To one portion, add food coloring; stir until uniform in color. In each muffin cup, place 2 Tbsp. red batter; top with 2 Tbsp. white batter. Swirl white batter through red batter with knife for marbled design.

3. Bake at 350° for 18 to 20 minutes or until a wooden pick inserted in center comes out clean. Cool in pans on wire racks 10 minutes; remove from pans to wire racks. Cool completely (about 30 minutes).

4. Frost cupcakes with frosting. Top each with crushed peppermint candies.

color wow!

Substitute green food coloring paste and green-and-white peppermint candies for a twist on this peppermint look. Or tint cake batter green, and use red-and-white peppermints for a Christmas theme.

layer by layer

flower stack cakes

MAKES 8 CAKES   Hands-On Time: 43 min.   Total Time: 3 hours, 13 min.

1 (15.25-oz.) package white cake mix

Water, vegetable oil, and egg whites
    called for on cake mix box

Teal food coloring paste

3/4 cup butter, softened

4 oz. cream cheese, softened

4 cups powdered sugar

1½ tsp. vanilla extract

1/8 tsp. yellow food coloring paste

Disposable decorating bag

1 Tbsp. edible white pearls

1. Preheat oven to 350°. Grease and flour 3 (9-inch) round cake pans. Prepare cake mix according to package directions, using water, oil, and egg whites. Divide batter evenly among 3 bowls (about 1½ cups batter per bowl). Tint 1 bowl with a dash of teal food coloring. Tint second bowl with 1/8 tsp. teal food coloring. Tint third bowl with ½ tsp. teal food coloring. Pour batter into prepared pans.

2. Bake at 350° for 18 to 20 minutes or until a wooden pick inserted in center comes out clean. Cool in pans on wire racks 10 minutes. Remove from pans to wire racks, and cool completely (about 1 hour).

3. Chill cakes for 1 hour. Cut darkest-colored cake layer into 8 flowers using a 2½-inch flower-shaped cutter. Cut medium-colored cake layer into 8 flowers using a 2-inch flower-shaped cutter. Cut lightest-colored cake layer into 8 flowers using a 1½-inch flower-shaped cutter. Reserve remaining cake for another use.

4. Beat butter and cream cheese at medium speed with an electric mixer until creamy; gradually add powdered sugar, beating at low speed until blended. Beat in vanilla; beat at medium speed 1 minute or until fluffy.

5. Tint ½ cup frosting with yellow food coloring. Spoon yellow frosting into a disposable decorating bag fitted with a leaf or petal tip. Pipe or spread remaining frosting between layers of cake rounds, stacking the darkest cake on the bottom and ending with the lightest cake. Pipe a flower on top with yellow frosting; sprinkle center of each flower with pearl candy.

peaches and cream mini ombre cakes

MAKES 12 SERVINGS   Hands-On Time: 45 min.   Total Time: 2 hours, 45 min.

Parchment paper
2 (15.25-oz.) packages yellow
    cake mix
Water, vegetable oil, and eggs called
    for on cake mix boxes
Peach food coloring gel
1½ cups whipping cream
2 Tbsp. powdered sugar
2 Tbsp. peach-flavored brandy
¾ cup peach jam
1 peach, peeled and sliced

1. Preheat oven to 325°. Lightly grease bottoms of 4 (13- x 9-inch) pans, and line with parchment paper. Prepare both packages of cake mix according to package directions, using water, oil, and eggs; divide batter into 4 equal portions in separate bowls. Pour 1 bowl batter into 1 prepared pan. Add dash of peach food coloring to second bowl of batter; stir until combined. Pour batter into second prepared pan. Add ⅛ tsp. peach food coloring to third bowl of batter; stir until combined. Pour batter into third prepared pan. Add ½ tsp. peach food coloring to remaining batter; stir until combined. Pour batter into remaining prepared pan.

2. Bake at 325° for 20 minutes or until a wooden pick inserted in center comes out clean. Cool in pans on wire racks 10 minutes; remove from pans to wire racks, and cool completely (about 30 minutes).

3. Beat whipping cream at high speed with an electric mixer until foamy; gradually add powdered sugar and brandy, beating until stiff peaks form.

4. Cut 12 circles from each cake layer with a 2½-inch round cutter. Place darkest-tinted circles on a serving platter; spread 1 tsp. peach jam and 2 tsp. whipped cream on top. Repeat process with remaining cake layers, jam, and whipped cream to make 12 (4-layer) cakes, stacking layers from darkest to lightest. Dollop whipped cream on tops of cake stacks. Cut 6 peach slices into quarters; reserve remaining peaches for another use. Top each with 2 peach pieces.

double berry-vanilla trifles

MAKES 16 SERVINGS   Hands-On Time: 18 min.   Total Time: 3 hours, 18 min.

Fresh berries and a homemade custard go nicely with a store-bought pound cake to create a speed-scratch dessert.

5 cups milk

1½ cups sugar

⅔ cup all-purpose flour

4 large egg yolks

1 Tbsp. vanilla extract

3 cups sliced fresh strawberries

3 cups fresh blueberries

1 cup strawberry preserves

1 tsp. lemon zest

1 (1-lb.) pound cake, cut into 1-inch
    cubes

1 cup sweetened whipped cream

Fresh blueberries

Fresh sliced strawberries

1. Whisk together first 4 ingredients in a medium-size heavy saucepan. Bring to a boil over medium heat, whisking constantly. Boil, whisking constantly, 5 to 6 minutes or until thickened. Remove pan from heat; stir in vanilla. Transfer warm custard to a large bowl and place heavy-duty plastic wrap directly on the surface (to prevent a film from forming); chill 3 hours.

2. Combine strawberries, blueberries, strawberry preserves, and lemon zest in a medium bowl.

3. Spoon one-third of custard (about 2 cups) into a 4-qt. trifle dish or evenly into individual glasses. Top with half of cake cubes and half of fruit mixture. Repeat layers once. Spoon remaining custard over fruit mixture. Top with sweetened whipped cream and additional blueberries and strawberries. Serve immediately, or cover and chill.

candy corn cupcake trifles

MAKES 12 SERVINGS   Hands-On Time: 25 min.   Total Time: 1 hour, 5 min.

Paper baking cups

1 (15.25-oz.) package vanilla cake mix with pudding

Water, vegetable oil, and eggs called for on cake mix box

½ tsp. orange food coloring paste

¼ tsp. yellow food coloring paste

12 (8-oz.) canning jars or other half-pint jars

2 (12-oz.) containers whipped ready-to-spread white frosting

1½ cups candy corn

1. Preheat oven to 350°. Place paper baking cups in 2 (12-cup) muffin pans. Prepare cake mix according to package directions, using water, oil, and eggs. Divide batter in half; tint half of batter orange and other half yellow. Spoon orange batter into 12 muffin cups and yellow batter into remaining muffin cups.

2. Bake at 350° for 18 to 20 minutes or until a wooden pick inserted in center comes out clean. Cool in pans on wire racks 10 minutes; remove from pans to wire racks. Cool completely (about 30 minutes).

3. Remove paper baking cups. Cut each cupcake in half horizontally. In each of 12 glass jars, place 1 yellow cupcake half and 1 orange cupcake half. Spoon 1 container of frosting into a large zip-top plastic freezer bag; seal bag. Cut off about ½-inch corner of bag. Squeeze bag to pipe frosting over orange cupcake in each jar. Divide 1 cup candy corn evenly among jars, and sprinkle over frosting. Repeat layers with remaining cupcake halves, second container of frosting, and remaining ½ cup candy corn.

simply smart

These treats are perfect for dessert on the go! Just assemble cakes in canning jars, and screw on lids to take to parties or picnics, or pack in lunch boxes.

strawberry swirl cream cheese pound cake

MAKES 12 SERVINGS   Hands-On Time: 25 min.   Total Time: 2 hours, 35 min.

1½ cups butter, softened

3 cups sugar

1 (8-oz.) package cream cheese, softened

6 large eggs

3 cups all-purpose flour

1 tsp. almond extract

½ tsp. vanilla extract

⅔ cup strawberry glaze

Garnish: fresh strawberries and sifted powdered sugar

1. Preheat oven to 350°. Grease and flour a 10-inch (14-cup) tube pan. Beat butter at medium speed with a heavy-duty electric stand mixer until creamy. Gradually add sugar, beating until light and fluffy. Add cream cheese, beating until creamy. Add eggs, 1 at a time, beating just until blended after each addition.

2. Gradually add flour to butter mixture. Beat at low speed just until blended after each addition, stopping to scrape bowl as needed. Stir in almond and vanilla extracts. Pour one-third of batter into prepared pan (about 2⅔ cups batter). Dollop 8 rounded teaspoonfuls strawberry glaze over batter, and swirl with wooden skewer. Repeat procedure once, and top with remaining third of batter.

3. Bake at 350° for 1 hour to 1 hour and 10 minutes or until a long wooden pick inserted in center comes out clean. Cool in pan on a wire rack 10 to 15 minutes; remove from pan to wire rack, and cool completely (about 1 hour).

Note: We tested with Marzetti Glaze for Strawberries.

color wow!

For this cake, the swirl of color is a surprise inside! Serve pound cake slices on a red platter or cake stand to play up the ruby strawberry hue.

green tea-honeysuckle cake

MAKES 12 SERVINGS   Hands-On Time: 30 min.   Total Time: 3 hours, 15 min., including glaze

1 cup butter, softened
½ cup shortening
2½ cups sugar
¼ cup honey
6 large eggs
3 cups all-purpose flour
1 tsp. baking powder
½ tsp. table salt
¾ cup milk
2 tsp. matcha (green tea powder)
Honeysuckle Glaze

honeysuckle glaze

Bring ¾ cup sugar, ½ cup butter, 1⅓ cups honey, ⅓ cup orange liqueur, and 3 Tbsp. water to a boil in a 1-qt. saucepan over medium heat, stirring often; reduce heat to medium-low, and boil, stirring constantly, 3 minutes. Makes about 1⅔ cups.

1. Preheat oven to 325°. Grease and flour a 14-cup Bundt pan. Beat butter and shortening at medium speed with a heavy-duty electric stand mixer until creamy. Gradually add sugar, beating until light and fluffy. Add honey, beating until blended. Add eggs, 1 at a time, beating just until blended after each addition.

2. Stir together flour and next 2 ingredients. Add to butter mixture alternately with milk, beginning and ending with flour mixture. Beat at low speed just until blended after each addition. Transfer 2½ cups batter to a 2-qt. bowl, and stir in matcha until blended.

3. Drop 2 scoops of plain batter into prepared pan, using a small cookie scoop (about 1½ inches); top with 1 scoop of matcha batter. Repeat procedure around entire pan, covering bottom completely. Continue layering batters in pan as directed until all batter is used.

4. Bake at 325° for 1 hour and 5 minutes to 1 hour and 15 minutes or until a long wooden pick inserted in center comes out clean.

5. During last 10 minutes of baking, prepare Honeysuckle Glaze. Remove cake from oven, and gradually spoon 1 cup hot Honeysuckle Glaze over cake in pan, allowing glaze to soak into cake after each addition. Reserve remaining glaze. Cool cake completely in pan on a wire rack (about 1 hour and 30 minutes).

6. Remove cake from pan; spoon reserved glaze over cake.

cherry limeade angel food cake

MAKES 10 TO 12 SERVINGS   Hands-On Time: 10 min.   Total Time: 3 hours

1 (16-oz.) package angel food cake mix, divided
3 Tbsp. lime-flavored gelatin
2 Tbsp. cherry-flavored gelatin
Garnishes: maraschino cherries and lime slices

1. Preheat oven to 350°. Divide cake mix into 2 large bowls.

2. To one bowl, add ½ cup plus 2 Tbsp. water; beat at high speed with an electric mixer 1 minute or until stiff peaks form. Reduce speed to medium; add lime-flavored gelatin, and beat just until combined. (Do not overbeat).

3. Wash beater. Add ½ cup plus 2 Tbsp. water to second bowl; beat at high speed with an electric mixer 1 minute or until stiff peaks form. Reduce speed to medium; add cherry-flavored gelatin, and beat just until combined. (Do not overbeat).

4. Carefully spoon about 1 cup of each batter into an ungreased 10-inch (16-cup) tube pan, alternating until both batters are used. Swirl batters gently with a knife.

5. Bake at 350° for 37 to 47 minutes or until top is deep golden brown and inside cracks feel dry. Immediately turn pan upside-down, and cool completely on a wire rack (about 2 hours). Gently run a small knife around inside edges of pan to release cake onto a serving plate.

color wow!

Try other flavored gelatins for different color and flavor options! For example, pink strawberry and yellow lemon are another winning pair.

tie-dyed poke cake

MAKES 15 SERVINGS   Hands-On Time: 35 min.   Total Time: 2 hours, 30 min.

Baking spray with flour

1 (15.25-oz.) package white cake mix

Water, vegetable oil, and egg whites
    called for on cake mix box

1 cup boiling water

3 Tbsp. each strawberry-flavored,
    lime-flavored, and berry blue-
    flavored gelatin (from 3-oz.
    packages)

1 (6-inch) wooden skewer

1 (12-oz.) container whipped ready-to-
    spread vanilla frosting

4 (0.68-oz.) tubes decorating gel
    (pink, green, orange, and blue)

1 fine-tip paintbrush

1. Preheat oven to 350°. Coat bottom only of a 13- x 9-inch pan with baking spray with flour. Prepare cake mix according to package directions for 13- x 9-inch pan, using water, oil, and egg whites. Bake as directed. Cool in pan on a wire rack 20 minutes.

2. Meanwhile, in three separate bowls, pour $\frac{1}{3}$ cup boiling water over each flavored gelatin; stir until gelatin is dissolved. Poke warm cake every inch with wooden skewer halfway into cake, twisting skewer back and forth. Pour each color gelatin randomly over cake, allowing gelatin to fill in holes. Cool completely (about 1 hour).

3. Frost cooled cake. With decorating gels, draw vertical lines $\frac{1}{4}$ inch apart on frosting, alternating colors. Pull fine-tip paintbrush in a straight line across all colors. Repeat, working back and forth from 1 side of cake to the other to create a tie-dyed effect.

spring berry poke cake

MAKES 15 SERVINGS   Hands-On Time: 20 min.   Total Time: 2 hours, 20 min.

2½ cups all-purpose flour
2 tsp. baking powder
½ tsp. table salt
¾ cup butter, softened
1½ cups sugar
1 tsp. vanilla extract
3 large eggs
1 cup milk
1 (3-oz.) package strawberry-flavored gelatin
1 cup boiling water
1 (12-oz.) container whipped ready-to-spread vanilla frosting
1 tsp. lemon zest
Garnish: 4 cups mixed fresh berries, fresh mint sprigs

1. Preheat oven to 350°. Grease bottom and sides of a 13- x 9-inch pan with shortening; lightly flour.

2. In medium bowl, mix flour, baking powder, and salt; set aside. In large bowl, beat butter, sugar, and vanilla at high speed with an electric mixer 3 minutes or until fluffy. Add eggs, 1 at a time, beating well after each addition. Add flour mixture alternately with milk, beating until blended after each addition and scraping bowl occasionally. Pour batter into prepared pan.

3. Bake at 350° for 35 to 40 minutes or until a wooden pick inserted in center comes out clean. Cool 20 minutes.

4. Meanwhile, in small bowl, stir together gelatin and boiling water 2 minutes to completely dissolve gelatin. Poke warm cake every inch with tines of meat fork or table knife. Pour strawberry mixture slowly over cake, allowing mixture to fill holes in cake. Cool completely in pan on wire rack (about 1 hour).

5. In small bowl, mix frosting and lemon zest. Frost cake.

color wow!

For a blue-and-white berry cake, substitute berry blue-flavored gelatin. Be prepared for a bold blueberry flavor!

halloween poke cake

MAKES 15 SERVINGS   Hands-On Time: 15 min.   Total Time: 2 hours, 10 min.

Cooking spray

1 (15.25-oz) package white cake mix with pudding

Water, vegetable oil, and egg whites called for on cake mix box

2 tsp. orange zest

1 cup boiling water

1 (3-oz.) package orange-flavored gelatin

1 (16-oz.) container ready-to-spread dark chocolate frosting

2 Tbsp. orange decorator sugar crystals

1. Preheat oven to 350°. Coat bottom only of a 13- x 9-inch pan with cooking spray. Prepare cake mix according to package directions, using water, oil, and egg whites and adding orange zest. Pour batter into prepared pan.

2. Bake at 350° for 27 to 32 minutes or until a wooden pick inserted in center comes out clean. Cool in pan on a wire rack 20 minutes.

3. Meanwhile, in small bowl, pour boiling water over gelatin; stir until gelatin is dissolved. Poke cake every inch with handle of wooden spoon or long skewer halfway into cake. Pour gelatin slowly over cake, allowing gelatin to fill holes. Cool completely (about 1 hour).

4. Frost cake. Sprinkle with sugar crystals. Store tightly covered in refrigerator.

simply smart

This cake features the classic combination of chocolate and orange. Grated orange zest in the cake batter intensifies the orange flavor.

rainbow
layer cake

MAKES 10 TO 12 SERVINGS   Hands-On Time: 1 hour, 15 min.   Total Time: 3 hours

Parchment paper

2 (15.25-oz.) packages white cake mix

Water, vegetable oil, and egg whites
    called for on cake mix boxes

Violet food coloring gel

Royal blue food coloring gel

Kelly green food coloring gel

Yellow food coloring gel

Orange food coloring gel

Red food coloring gel

3 (16-oz.) cans ready-to-spread
    vanilla frosting, divided

2¾ cups powdered sugar, divided

1. Preheat oven to 350°. Grease 6 (8-inch) round cake pans; line with parchment paper. Prepare double batch of cake mix according to package directions, using water, oil, and egg whites. Divide batter evenly between 6 bowls. Stir ⅛ tsp. each of violet, blue, green, and yellow coloring into 4 of the batters. Stir ½ to 1 tsp. orange into the fifth bowl, and ¾ to 1 tsp. red coloring into the sixth bowl. Pour batters into prepared pans.

2. Bake cake layers at 350° for 13 to 15 minutes or until a wooden pick inserted in center comes out clean. Cool in pans on wire racks 10 minutes; remove cakes from pans to wire racks, and cool completely (about 1 hour).

3. Beat 2 cans frosting with 1 cup powdered sugar at medium speed with an electric mixer until light and fluffy (2 to 3 minutes). Stack cake layers with ⅓ cup frosting in between each layer. With 1¼ cups frosting, spread a thin layer of frosting on top and sides of cakes.

4. Add remaining can of frosting and remaining 1¾ cups powdered sugar to remaining frosting in bowl. Beat at medium speed with electric mixer until light and fluffy (2 to 3 minutes). Divide frosting into 3 bowls. Tint 2 bowls different shades of light blue. Frost cake with deepest blue toward the bottom and white frosting on top. Use back of spoon to blend and swirl frosting.

strawberries and cream cake

MAKES 12 SERVINGS
Hands-On Time: 30 min.   Total Time: 22 hours, 10 min., including filling and frosting

2 cups sifted cake flour
2 ½ tsp. baking powder
½ tsp. table salt
3 ¾ cups sugar, divided
½ cup canola oil
¼ cup fresh lemon juice
4 large egg yolks
8 large egg whites
1 tsp. cream of tartar
4 cups mashed strawberries
1 (3-oz.) package strawberry-
    flavored gelatin
Strawberry Frosting

strawberry frosting

Stir together 1 Tbsp. strawberry-flavored gelatin and 2 Tbsp. boiling water in a small bowl; cool completely (about 20 minutes). Beat 1 cup whipping cream and gelatin mixture at high speed with an electric mixer until foamy; gradually add ¼ cup sugar, beating until soft peaks form. Stir in 1 (8-oz.) container sour cream, ¼ cup at a time, stirring just until blended after each addition.

1. Preheat oven to 350°. Stir together first 3 ingredients and 1 cup sugar in a large bowl. Make a well in center of mixture; add oil, next 2 ingredients, and ¼ cup water. Beat at medium-high speed with an electric mixer 3 to 4 minutes or until smooth.

2. Beat egg whites and cream of tartar at medium-high speed until soft peaks form. Gradually add ¼ cup sugar, 1 Tbsp. at a time, beating until stiff peaks form. Gently fold one-fourth of egg white mixture into flour mixture; gently fold in remaining egg white mixture. Pour batter into 6 greased and floured 8-inch round cake pans.

3. Bake at 350° for 12 to 15 minutes or until a wooden pick inserted in center comes out clean. Cool in pans on wire racks 10 minutes; remove from pans to wire racks, and cool completely (about 1 hour).

4. Stir together strawberries and remaining 2 ½ cups sugar in a large saucepan; let stand 30 minutes. Bring strawberry mixture to a boil over medium heat; boil 5 minutes. Remove from heat, and stir in gelatin until dissolved; cool completely (about 1 hour). Cover and chill 8 hours.

5. Spread filling between cake layers, leaving a ¼-inch border around edges (about ⅔ cup filling between each layer). Cover cake with plastic wrap, and chill 8 to 24 hours. Spread Strawberry Frosting on top and sides of cake. Chill 2 hours before serving.

orange ombre cake

MAKES 14 TO 16 SERVINGS   Hands-On Time: 45 min.   Total Time: 2 hours, 20 min.

Parchment paper
2 (15.25-oz.) packages white cake mix
Water, vegetable oil, and egg whites
    called for on cake mix boxes
¼ cup thawed, frozen orange juice
    concentrate
1 Tbsp. orange zest
Orange food coloring paste
Sweet Orange Frosting

sweet orange frosting

Beat 2¼ cups softened, salted butter at medium speed with an electric mixer until creamy; gradually add 8 cups powdered sugar, beating until blended. Beat in ⅓ cup frozen orange juice concentrate (thawed), ½ tsp. vanilla extract and 1 Tbsp. orange zest. Beat at medium speed 2 minutes or until light and fluffy.

1. Preheat oven to 350°. Grease 4 (8-inch) round cake pans; line with parchment paper. Prepare double batch of cake mix according to package directions, using water, oil, and egg whites and adding ¼ cup orange juice concentrate and 1 Tbsp. orange zest. Divide batter evenly among 4 bowls (about 2½ cups per bowl).

2. Set 1 bowl aside. Add dash orange food coloring to second bowl, stirring until blended. Color batters in remaining 2 bowls gradually darker shades of orange. Spoon batter into prepared pans.

3. Bake at 350° for 22 to 24 minutes or until a wooden pick inserted in center comes out clean. Cool in pans on wire racks 10 minutes; remove from pans to wire racks, and cool completely (about 1 hour).

4. Set aside 1 cup Sweet Orange Frosting in a small bowl. Divide remaining 6 cups frosting evenly among 3 bowls. Add dash of orange food coloring paste to one bowl, stirring until blended. Color remaining 2 bowls of frosting gradually darker shades of orange.

5. Place darkest orange cake layer on a cake stand. Spread 1 cup darkest orange frosting evenly over cake. Repeat process with cake layers and frosting, layering from darkest to lightest. Spread remaining darkest-tinted orange frosting on bottom third of cake sides. Spread remaining medium-tinted frosting on middle third of cake sides. Spread remaining lightest-tinted frosting on top third of cake sides. Spread plain frosting on top of cake.

Step 1

Step 3

Step 4

polka dot
cake

MAKES 12 SERVINGS   Hands-On Time: 40 min.   Total Time: 2 hours, 15 min.

Parchment paper
2 (15.25-oz.) packages white cake mix
Water, vegetable oil, and egg whites
    called for on cake mix boxes
Purple food coloring paste
Pink food coloring paste
Lime green food coloring paste
Blue food coloring paste
3 (12-oz.) containers whipped ready-
    to-spread white frosting

1. Preheat oven to 350°. Grease cavities of 1 cake pop mold and 3 (8-inch) round cake pans; line round cake pans with parchment paper. Prepare double batch of cake mix according to package directions, using water, oil, and egg whites. Divide 2 cups batter evenly among 4 bowls; refrigerate remaining white batter. Tint batters purple, pink, green, and blue with food coloring. Spoon ⅓ of each colored batter into prepared cake pop molds; refrigerate remaining batter.

2. Bake at 350° for 7 to 9 minutes or until a wooden pick inserted in center comes out clean. Immediately remove from pans, and cool completely on a wire rack. Wash cake pop molds, and repeat procedure twice.

3. Place 3 cake balls of each color into each cake pan. Spoon reserved white batter over cake balls in prepared pans, covering cake balls completely. Bake 23 to 25 minutes or until a wooden pick inserted in center comes out clean. Cool in pans on wire racks 10 minutes; remove from pans to wire racks, and cool completely (about 1 hour).

4. Divide frosting into 4 bowls. Tint frosting purple, pink, green, and blue with food coloring. Spread frosting, alternating colors, between layers and on top and sides of cake.

Resource Note: Look for a 12-cavity cake pop pan online or at crafts stores.

raspberries-and-cream layer cake

MAKES 14 TO 16 SERVINGS   Hands-On Time: 45 min.   Total Time: 3 hours, 15 min.

2½ cups cake flour

2 Tbsp. unsweetened cocoa

1 tsp. baking soda

1 cup buttermilk

2 (1-oz.) bottles red food coloring

1 Tbsp. cider vinegar

1 tsp. vanilla extract

1½ cups butter, softened and divided

1½ cups sugar

3 large eggs

1 (15.25-oz.) package white cake mix

Water, vegetable oil, and egg whites called for on cake mix box

¾ cup seedless red raspberry jam

5 Tbsp. raspberry-flavored liqueur or syrup, divided

Cream Cheese Frosting

Garnish: 2 cups fresh raspberries

cream cheese frosting

In large bowl, beat 2 (8-oz.) packages softened cream cheese and ½ cup softened butter at medium speed until light and fluffy. On low speed, beat in 2 tsp. vanilla extract. Gradually beat in 8 cups powdered sugar until mixed; beat on medium speed until fluffy.

1. Preheat oven to 350°. Grease and flour bottoms only of 4 (9-inch) round cake pans. In medium bowl, mix flour, cocoa, and baking soda. In 2-cup glass measuring cup, mix buttermilk, food coloring, vinegar, and vanilla. In large bowl, beat 1 cup butter and sugar at medium speed with an electric mixer 2 minutes or until creamy. Add 3 eggs, 1 at a time, beating well after each addition. Alternately add flour mixture with buttermilk mixture, beating at low speed until blended. Pour batter evenly into 2 of the pans.

2. Bake at 350° for 35 minutes or until a wooden pick inserted in center comes out clean. Cool 10 minutes; remove from pans to wire racks. Cool completely.

3. Prepare cake mix according to package directions, using water, oil, and egg whites. Pour batter into remaining 2 pans. Bake at 350° for 25 minutes or until a wooden pick inserted in center comes out clean. Cool 10 minutes; remove from pans to wire racks. Cool completely (about 1 hour). In bowl, mix jam and 1 Tbsp. liqueur.

4. Using serrated knife, cut rounded top off each white cake to level surface. Cut each red velvet cake horizontally to make 2 layers. Brush off loose crumbs. Place 1 red velvet cake layer, cut side up, on serving plate; brush with 2 Tbsp. liqueur. Spread with half of raspberry jam mixture. Top with 1 white cake; spread with ¾ cup Cream Cheese Frosting. Repeat layers. Top with a third red velvet cake layer. (Reserve remaining red velvet cake layer for another use.) Spread very thin layer of frosting on side of cake to seal in crumbs. Spread remaining frosting on top and sides of cake.

Step 2

Step 3

Step 4

patriotic checkerboard cake

MAKES 16 SERVINGS   Hands-On Time: 45 min.   Total Time: 4 hours, 20 min.

Parchment paper
2 (15.25-oz.) packages white cake mix
Water, vegetable oil, and egg whites
    called for on cake mix boxes
Royal blue food coloring paste
3 (12-oz.) containers ready-to-spread
    fluffy white frosting
Red food coloring paste
Fondant Stars

fondant stars

Place ¼ (24-oz.) package rolled fondant on a surface lightly dusted with powdered sugar, and roll to ⅛-inch thickness. Cut with various-size star-shaped cookie cutters. Place stars on a parchment paper-lined baking sheet; sprinkle with sparkling sugar, and dry completely (4 hours to overnight).

1. Preheat oven to 350°. Grease 3 (9-inch) round cake pans, and line bottoms with parchment paper. Prepare double batch of cake mix according to package directions, using water, oil, and egg whites. Transfer 5½ cups batter to one bowl; stir in 1 tsp. royal blue food coloring.

2. Place checkerboard ring into one prepared pan. Spoon blue batter into outer ring and center, filling three-fourths full. Spoon white batter into middle ring. Gently lift out checkerboard ring, and wash. Repeat process with second prepared pan. Repeat process with third pan but changing the order of blue and white batter.

3. Bake at 350° for 25 to 27 minutes or until a wooden pick inserted in center comes out clean. Cool in pans on wire racks 10 minutes; remove from pans to wire racks, and cool completely (about 1 hour). Level cake layers with a serrated knife.

4. Place cake layer with blue outer ring on a cake plate; spread about ⅔ cup frosting over top of cake layer. Place cake layer with white outer ring on top; spread about ⅔ cup frosting over top of cake layer. Place remaining cake layer on top; spread top and sides of cake with 1½ cups frosting.

5. Divide remaining white frosting evenly between 3 bowls. Tint 1 bowl frosting with ½ tsp. royal blue food coloring. Tint second bowl with 1 tsp. red food coloring, leaving third bowl white. Decorate cake with red, white, and blue frosting. Top cake with Fondant Stars.

present cake

MAKES 14 TO 16 SERVINGS   Hands-On Time: 55 min.   Total Time: 3 hours, 5 min.

2 (15.25-oz.) packages vanilla
   cake mix
2 cups milk
1 cup vegetable oil
6 large eggs
1½ tsp. almond extract
½ cup seedless strawberry jam
4 (12-oz.) containers ready-to-spread
   cream cheese frosting
1 (4.5-oz.) package strawberry chewy
   fruit snack rolls
3 (0.5-oz.) packages candy buttons

1. Preheat oven to 350°. Grease 3 (8-inch) square pans with shortening; lightly flour.

2. In large bowl, beat cake mixes, milk, oil, eggs, and almond extract at low speed with an electric mixer 30 seconds, then at medium speed 2 minutes. Divide batter evenly among pans.

3. Bake at 350° for 25 to 30 minutes or until a wooden pick inserted in center comes out clean. Cool in pans on wire racks 10 minutes; remove from pans to wire racks. Cool completely (about 1 hour).

4. With serrated knife, level top of each cake layer. Place 1 cake layer, cut side up, on serving plate; spread with ¼ cup jam. Spread ¾ cup frosting over jam. Repeat with second cake layer, cut side up, ¼ cup jam, and ¾ cup frosting. Top with remaining cake layer, cut side down. Carefully spread thin layer of frosting over sides and top of cake. Refrigerate 30 minutes. Apply second thicker layer of frosting to sides and top of cake, spreading until smooth.

5. Cut 4 (8-inch) pieces from fruit snacks. Place on top and sides of cake, pressing gently into frosting to look like ribbon. Spoon ¼ cup frosting in mound on center of cake. Cut remaining fruit snacks into 4-inch pieces. Fold each piece in half to look like loops of bow; press into frosting mound to create a large bow. Decorate cake with candy buttons.

Note: We tested with Necco® Candy Buttons.

raspberry-lime rickey cake

MAKES 20 SERVINGS   Hands-On Time: 42 min.   Total Time: 2 hours, 28 min.

This cake mimics the flavors of a signature summer drink made with raspberry syrup, fresh lime juice, and seltzer.

Parchment paper

2 (15.25-oz.) packages white cake mix

Water, vegetable oil, and egg whites called for on cake mix boxes

1/4 cup raspberry-flavored gelatin, divided

1/4 cup lime-flavored gelatin, divided

2 1/2 cups butter, softened

8 cups powdered sugar

7 Tbsp. frozen limeade concentrate, thawed

1/8 tsp. green food coloring paste

Garnishes: fresh raspberries, thin lime slices

1. Preheat oven to 350°. Grease 3 (9-inch) round cake pans; line bottoms with parchment paper.

2. Prepare 1 package cake mix according to package directions, using water, oil, and egg whites. Divide batter evenly into each of three bowls. Add 2 Tbsp. raspberry gelatin to 1 bowl; pour batter into 1 prepared cake pan. Add 2 Tbsp. lime gelatin to another bowl; pour batter into 1 prepared cake pan. Pour remaining batter into remaining cake pan. Bake at 350° for 18 minutes or until a wooden pick inserted in center comes out clean. Cool in pans on wire racks 10 minutes; remove from pans to wire racks, and cool completely (about 1 hour). Wash and dry pans; repeat with remaining cake mix and gelatin.

3. Beat butter at low speed with an electric mixer until creamy; gradually add powdered sugar, beating well. Add limeade concentrate and food coloring; beat until blended. Increase speed to medium-high, and beat until light and fluffy.

4. Place 1 lime cake layer onto serving platter; spread evenly with 1/2 cup frosting. Top with 1 white cake layer; spread evenly with 1/2 cup frosting. Top with 1 raspberry cake layer; spread evenly with 1/2 cup frosting. Repeat process with remaining cake layers and 1 1/2 cups frosting. Spread remaining 2 1/2 cups frosting over top and sides of cake.

neapolitan confetti cake

MAKES 14 TO 16 SERVINGS   Hands-On Time: 1 hour, 30 min.   Total Time: 3 hours, 15 min.

4 cups all-purpose flour

6 tsp. baking powder

1 tsp. table salt

1½ cups milk

2 tsp. vanilla extract

1 tsp. almond extract

9 large egg whites

1¼ cups butter, softened

2½ cups sugar

½ cup chopped fresh strawberries

Pink food coloring paste

1 (4-oz.) semisweet chocolate baking
    bar, melted and cooled

3 (12-oz.) containers whipped ready-
    to-spread white frosting

½ cup seedless strawberry jam

6 oz. white rolled fondant
    (from 24-oz. box)

3 oz. chocolate-flavored rolled
    fondant (from 24-oz. box)

1. Preheat oven to 350°. Grease bottoms and sides of 3 (9-inch) round cake pans with shortening; lightly flour. In small bowl, mix flour, baking powder, and salt. In medium bowl, stir milk, vanilla and almond extracts, and egg whites with whisk until well blended. In large bowl, beat butter and sugar at medium speed with an electric mixer 5 minutes or until light and fluffy. Add flour mixture alternately with milk mixture, beating at low speed after each addition just until smooth.

2. Divide batter into 3 bowls. Stir strawberries and desired amount of pink food coloring into one bowl; stir melted chocolate into second bowl; leave third bowl white. Pour batters into prepared cake pans. Bake at 350° for 30 to 35 minutes or until a wooden pick inserted in center comes out clean. Cool in pans on wire racks 10 minutes; remove cakes from pans to wire racks. Cool completely (about 1 hour).

3. In large bowl, beat together frosting, jam, and desired amount of pink food coloring until blended and smooth. Place chocolate cake layer on serving plate; spread with about 1 cup frosting. Top with white cake layer; spread with about 1 cup frosting. Top with strawberry cake layer. Spread remaining frosting on top and sides of cake.

4. Divide white fondant in half. Tint half of white fondant with pink food coloring, kneading until smooth. Place pink fondant on a surface lightly coated with powdered sugar, and roll to ⅛-inch thickness. Cut with various-size round cutters. Place on cake. Repeat process with white and chocolate fondant.

psychedelic layer cake

MAKES 14 TO 16 SERVINGS   Hands-On Time: 25 min.   Total Time: 1 hour, 52 min.

Parchment paper

2 (15.25-oz.) packages white cake mix

Water, vegetable oil, and egg whites called for on cake mix boxes

¼ tsp. pink food coloring paste

¼ tsp. blue food coloring paste

¼ tsp. electric green food coloring paste

¼ tsp. yellow food coloring paste

3 (12-oz.) containers ready-to-spread fluffy white frosting

1. Preheat oven to 350°. Grease 4 (8-inch) round cake pans; line with parchment paper.

2. Prepare double batch of cake mix according to package directions, using water, oil, and egg whites. Divide batter evenly between 4 bowls (about 2½ heaping cups batter per bowl). Tint one bowl with pink food coloring. Tint second bowl with blue food coloring. Tint third bowl with electric green food coloring. Tint fourth bowl with yellow food coloring.

3. Drop batter by ½ cupfuls into prepared pans, alternating colors. Swirl batter gently with a knife.

4. Bake at 350° for 22 minutes or until a wooden pick inserted in center comes out clean. Cool in pans on wire racks 10 minutes; remove from pans to wire racks, and cool completely (about 40 minutes).

5. Level cake layers by trimming with a serrated knife. Divide frosting into 4 bowls, and tint each bowl a different color. Spread frosting between layers. Frost cake in small sections with alternating colors. Once completely frosted, swirl edges of colors together using the back of a small spoon.

lemon-cherry cheesecake

MAKES 16 SERVINGS   Hands-On Time: 25 min.   Total Time: 11 hours, 15 min.

This cheesecake is not just creamy and delicious, it also has a surprise inside—cherry pie filling!

1¼ cups graham cracker crumbs
    (about 10 sheets)
¼ cup butter, melted
1⅓ cups plus ¼ cup sugar, divided
Cooking spray
3 (8-oz.) packages cream cheese,
    softened
6 large eggs
1 (16-oz.) container sour cream
¼ cup all-purpose flour
2 Tbsp. lemon zest
2 Tbsp. fresh lemon juice
2 tsp. vanilla extract
Lemon yellow food coloring paste
1¼ cups cherry pie filling
1 (2.9-oz.) package lemon cook-and-
    serve pudding mix

1. Preheat oven to 350°. Stir together graham cracker crumbs, butter, and ¼ cup sugar. Press mixture on bottom and up sides of a 10-inch springform pan coated with cooking spray. Bake at 350° for 10 minutes. Cool on a wire rack. Reduce oven temperature to 325°.

2. Beat cream cheese and remaining 1⅓ cups sugar at medium speed with an electric mixer until blended. Add eggs, 1 at a time, beating just until yellow disappears after each addition. Add sour cream, flour, lemon zest, lemon juice, and vanilla, beating at low speed until well blended. Tint batter light yellow with lemon yellow food coloring. Pour 4 cups batter into prepared crust; chill remaining batter.

3. Bake at 325° for 50 minutes or until center is almost set. Remove from oven, and gently top cheesecake with cherry pie filling to within 1 inch of edges. Top pie filling with remaining batter. Bake 45 more minutes or until almost set. Turn oven off. Let cheesecake stand in oven with door closed 1 hour. Remove cheesecake from oven, and gently run a sharp knife around outer edge of cheesecake to loosen from sides of pan. (Do not remove sides of pan.) Cool on a wire rack 1 hour. Cover and chill 8 hours.

4. Remove sides of pan. Prepare lemon pudding according to package directions; spread over cheesecake.

cookie
jar

surprise cherry cookies

MAKES 24 SERVINGS   Hands-On Time: 18 min.   Total Time: 43 min.

These mini muffin-shaped cookies have a surprise cherry center and lots of almond flavor.

1 (17.5-oz.) package sugar cookie mix
24 whole red maraschino cherries
    with stems, drained and patted
    dry
1½ cups powdered sugar
5 tsp. milk
⅛ tsp. almond extract
1 Tbsp. rainbow candy sprinkles

1. Preheat oven to 375°. Prepare cookie dough according to package directions.

2. Shape dough into 24 balls. Flatten each ball into a disc, and wrap around each cherry, covering completely and sealing edges. Place dough balls into 2 lightly greased (12-cup) miniature muffin pans. Bake at 375° for 12 minutes or until lightly browned and just firm. Cool in pans on wire racks 5 minutes. Transfer to wire racks, and cool completely.

3. Whisk together powdered sugar, milk, and almond extract until smooth, adding additional milk, if necessary, for desired glaze consistency. Spoon glaze onto each cookie; top with candy sprinkles.

simply smart

These cookie cups make great gifts! Place them in paper cupcake liners and wrap in cellophane, or nestle them into a small tin wrapped with ribbon.

bunny cookie cups

MAKES 12 SERVINGS   Hands-On Time: 35 min.   Total Time: 1 hour, 25 min.

Get your party "hopping" with these springtime strawberry-flavored cookie cups. Serve them nestled in Easter grass on a party tray or in a basket!

Cooking spray

1 (16-oz.) package refrigerated ready-to-bake sugar cookie dough (24 cookies)

2 Tbsp. granulated sugar

1 cup frozen whipped topping, thawed

½ cup finely chopped fresh strawberries

1 (12-oz.) container whipped ready-to-spread strawberry frosting

Disposable decorating bag

6 jumbo marshmallows

2 Tbsp. pink sparkling sugar

24 semisweet chocolate mini-morsels

12 heart-shaped red candies

1 pink sour candy belt or chewy fruit roll, cut into strips

1 (7-oz.) pouch chocolate brownie icing

1. Preheat oven to 350°. Spray 12 muffin cups with cooking spray. Place 2 cookie dough rounds in each cup, pressing in bottoms and up sides to form shells.

2. Bake at 350° for 24 minutes or until golden brown (dough will puff). For each cookie cup, dip end of wooden spoon handle in sugar; carefully press into bottom of cup to reshape. Cool in pan on wire rack 5 minutes; remove from pan to wire rack. Cool completely (about 15 minutes).

3. Mix whipped topping and strawberries; divide among cookie cups. Spoon frosting into decorating bag fitted with ½-inch round tip; pipe over filling. Cut each marshmallow into 4 slices; sprinkle cut sides with pink sugar. Press slices into frosting for ears. Add chocolate mini-morsels for eyes, red candy for nose, and pink candy strips for whiskers. Pipe with chocolate icing for mouth.

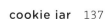

sugar cookie
fruit cups

MAKES 12 SERVINGS   Hands-On Time: 20 min.   Total Time: 1 hour, 5 min.

Paper baking cups
1 (16-oz.) package refrigerated
     ready-to-bake sugar cookie
     dough (24 cookies)
2 Tbsp. granulated sugar
1 (3.88-oz.) snack-size container
     vanilla pudding
¼ cup sour cream
1 Tbsp. brown sugar
1 cup sliced fresh peaches
1 cup fresh raspberries
1 cup fresh cherries, pitted and halved
1 cup sliced fresh strawberries
⅓ cup orange marmalade, melted
Garnish: fresh mint leaves

1. Preheat oven to 350°. Place paper baking cups in 1 (12-cup) muffin pan. Place 2 cookie dough rounds in each cup, pressing in bottoms and up sides to form shells.

2. Bake at 350° for 24 minutes or until golden brown (dough will puff). For each cookie cup, dip end of wooden spoon handle in sugar; carefully press into bottom of cup to reshape. Cool in pan on a wire rack 5 minutes; remove from pan to wire rack. Cool completely (about 15 minutes).

3. In small bowl, mix pudding, sour cream, and brown sugar. Divide pudding mixture evenly among cookie cups. (Cups will not be full.)

4. In medium bowl, mix blueberries, raspberries, and blackberries. Drizzle melted marmalade over fruit; stir gently to coat. Divide fruit evenly among cookie cups.

simply
smart

A light
coating of orange
marmalade gives fruit a
glossy finish and protects
it from drying out.

strawberry madeleines

MAKES 24 SERVINGS   Hands-On Time: 15 min.   Total Time: 50 min.

Using cake mix is the secret to making these fancy tea-time treats with ease.

1 cup strawberry cake mix
¼ cup milk
¼ cup butter, melted
½ tsp. lemon zest
1 large egg
1 cup powdered sugar
2 Tbsp. lemon juice
Garnish: white candy sprinkles

1. Preheat oven to 375°. Beat first 5 ingredients at medium speed with an electric mixer 2 minutes. Spoon about 1½ Tbsp. batter into each well of 2 lightly greased, shiny madeleine pans, filling two-thirds full.

2. Bake at 375° for 6 to 8 minutes or until centers of madeleines spring back when lightly touched. Immediately remove from pans to wire racks, and cool completely (about 20 minutes).

3. Whisk together powdered sugar and lemon juice in a small bowl. Dip madeleines in glaze; place on a wire rack, and let stand 10 minutes or until glaze is set.

simply smart

Store any remaining cake mix in a zip-top plastic storage bag to have on hand for baking these pink madeleines anytime.

pistachio
macarons

MAKES 36 SERVINGS   Hands-On Time: 45 min.   Total Time: 4 hours, 15 min.

1¼ cups shelled unsalted pistachios

1½ cups powdered sugar

4 large egg whites, room temperature

Pinch of cream of tartar

Pinch of table salt

½ cup granulated sugar

Leaf green food coloring paste

3 large (16-inch) disposable
    decorating bags

Parchment paper

Bittersweet Chocolate Ganache

bittersweet chocolate ganache

Chop 8 oz. bittersweet chocolate, and place in a medium bowl. Bring ¾ cup whipping cream to a boil in a small saucepan over medium heat. Pour over chocolate; let stand 1 minute. Whisk until smooth. Place plastic wrap directly on surface of ganache; chill 1 to 2 hours or until thickened.

1. Pulse pistachios and powdered sugar in a food processor 1 minute or until very finely ground.

2. Beat egg whites and cream of tartar at high speed with an electric mixer until foamy; add salt. Gradually add granulated sugar, 1 Tbsp. at a time, beating until stiff peaks almost form and sugar dissolves. Fold in ground pistachio mixture in three intervals until just combined and batter is the consistency of thick lava. Divide batter evenly among 3 bowls.

3. Stir ⅛ tsp. food coloring into batter of 1 bowl. Dab food coloring with a toothpick, and stir into batter of second bowl to create a medium shade of green. Dab a smaller amount of food coloring paste with a toothpick to create a lighter shade of green.

4. Spoon batters into each of 3 disposable decorating bags fitted with a ½-inch round tip. Pipe batters into 1½-inch rounds ½ inch apart onto 3 parchment paper-lined baking sheets. Let stand 1 hour before baking.

5. Preheat oven to 300°. Tap 1 baking sheet on counter, and place on lowest rack in oven. Bake at 300°, 1 baking sheet at a time, 15 minutes or until macarons are dry and release easily from parchment paper. Cool completely on baking sheets (about 30 minutes).

6. Spoon Bittersweet Chocolate Ganache into a zip-top plastic freezer bag. Snip 1 corner of bag to make a hole (about ¼ inch in diameter). Pipe ganache onto flat sides of half of macarons; top with remaining macarons, flat sides down.

Step 4

Step 6

Step 6

purple-packed sandwich cookies

MAKES 28 SERVINGS   Hands-On Time: 50 min.   Total Time: 1 hour, 10 min.

1 (16.25-oz.) package white cake mix

½ cup vegetable oil

¼ cup milk

2 large eggs

⅓ cup purple candy sprinkles

Parchment paper

⅔ cup butter, softened

2 cups powdered sugar

½ tsp. vanilla extract

½ tsp. purple food coloring paste

1. Preheat oven to 350°. In large bowl, beat cake mix, oil, milk, and eggs at medium speed with an electric mixer 2 minutes or until blended. Stir in sprinkles. Drop batter by level tablespoonfuls 2 inches apart onto parchment paper-lined baking sheets to yield 56 cookies.

2. Bake at 350° for 10 to 12 minutes or until set. Cool 5 minutes; remove from baking sheets to wire racks. Cool completely (about 20 minutes).

3. In large bowl, beat butter and powdered sugar at medium speed with an electric mixer 2 minutes or until light and fluffy. Beat in vanilla and food coloring until blended. For each sandwich cookie, spread about 1 Tbsp. frosting on bottom of 1 cookie. Top with second cookie, bottom side down; gently press together.

color wow!

Give these sandwich cookies a bigger punch of purple by sprinkling additional purple sprinkles over tops of cookies before baking.

orange sandwich cookies

MAKES 18 SERVINGS   Hands-On Time: 24 min.   Total Time: 1 hour, 4 min.

Get a double dose of orange in color and in flavor plus
a thick, creamy frosting sandwiched in the middle.

1 (17.5-oz.) pouch sugar cookie mix

1 cup butter, softened and divided

1 large egg

1 tsp. orange zest

1/4 tsp. orange food coloring paste

1/2 cup orange decorator sugar
    crystals

1 tsp. vanilla extract

2 1/3 cups powdered sugar

1/4 tsp. yellow food coloring paste

1. Preheat oven to 350°. Stir together cookie mix, 1/2 cup butter, egg, orange zest, and food coloring until well blended. Shape dough into 1-inch balls; roll in sugar crystals to coat. Place 2 inches apart on ungreased baking sheets.

2. Bake at 350° for 10 minutes or until set. Cool on baking sheets 5 minutes. Transfer to wire racks, and cool completely (about 30 minutes).

3. Beat remaining 1/2 cup butter and vanilla at medium speed with an electric mixer until creamy. Gradually add powdered sugar, 1/2 cup at a time, beating until blended after each addition and stopping to scrape bowl as needed. Stir in yellow food coloring until well blended.

4. Spread about 1 Tbsp. frosting on flat side of half of cookies. Top with remaining cookies, pressing gently.

Step 2

Step 2

Step 3

tie-dyed cookies

MAKES 48 SERVINGS   Hands-On Time: 30 min.   Total Time: 4 hours

2 (18-oz.) packages refrigerated sugar
    cookie dough
½ cup all-purpose flour, divided
Red, royal blue, leaf green, and lemon
    yellow food coloring pastes
Parchment paper

1. Divide each package of cookie dough into 2 equal portions. Knead 2 Tbsp. flour into each portion of dough. Knead $\frac{1}{16}$ tsp. red food coloring into 1 portion of dough, $\frac{1}{16}$ tsp. royal blue food coloring into second portion dough, $\frac{1}{16}$ tsp. leaf green food coloring into third portion, and $\frac{1}{16}$ tsp. lemon yellow food coloring into fourth portion. Shape each portion into a 4-inch square. Cover and chill 1 hour.

2. Stack 2 dough squares, and roll into a 12- x 10-inch rectangle between 2 pieces of parchment paper. Repeat with remaining 2 squares. Stack rectangles, and trim edges to a 12- x 9-inch rectangle. Press down handle of a wooden spoon lengthwise along dough to make 8 indentations, about 1 inch apart. Roll dough into a 12-inch log. Wrap in plastic wrap, and freeze 2 hours or until very firm.

3. Preheat oven to 350°. Unwrap dough, and cut into ¼-inch-thick slices. Place cookies 2 inches apart on ungreased baking sheets. Bake at 350° 10 minutes or until set. Cool on baking sheets 5 minutes. Transfer to wire racks to cool completely.

simply smart

Be sure to roll up the layered and indented dough very tightly so that the "tie-dyed" look is the clearest.

rainbow
iced cookies

MAKES 16 SERVINGS   Hands-On Time: 30 min.   Total Time: 1 hour, 20 min.

1 (17.5-oz.) pouch sugar cookie mix

Butter and egg called for on
    cookie mix pouch

1 (16-oz.) container ready-to-spread
    vanilla frosting

1 drop light blue food coloring

6 (4.25-oz.) tubes decorating icing
    (red, orange, yellow, green, blue,
    and purple)

Disposable decorating bag

White sanding sugar (optional)

1. Preheat oven to 375°. In a large bowl, stir cookie mix, butter, and egg until dough forms. On lightly floured surface, roll dough to ¼-inch thickness. Cut with 3-inch round cutter. Place cutouts about 2 inches apart on ungreased baking sheets.

2. Bake at 375° for 9 to 11 minutes or until edges are golden brown. Cool 2 minutes; remove from baking sheets to wire racks, and cool completely.

3. In small bowl, mix 1 cup vanilla frosting and the blue food coloring. Frost cookies. Let stand 10 minutes. With decorating icings, pipe thick stripes of each color for rainbow. Spoon remaining vanilla frosting into decorating bag fitted with ½-inch round tip. Pipe clouds onto cookies. Sprinkle with white sanding sugar, if desired. Let stand until set.

simply smart

Letting the icing set before adding rainbow stripes is the trick that gives the rainbow a three-dimensional look.

striped peppermint cookies

MAKES 64 COOKIES   Hands-On Time: 30 min.   Total Time: 3 hours

1 cup butter, softened
1 cup sugar
1 large egg
½ tsp. peppermint extract
2¼ cups all-purpose flour
¼ tsp. table salt
1 tsp. red food coloring paste

1. Line an 8- x 4-inch loaf pan with plastic wrap, allowing wrap to extend 1 inch over sides of pan. In large bowl, beat butter and sugar at medium speed with an electric mixer until light and fluffy. Add egg and peppermint extract, and beat just until blended. On medium-low speed, beat in flour and salt until blended.

2. Divide dough in half. Tint half of dough with red food coloring, kneading with gloved hands until well blended. Press half of plain dough evenly in bottom of pan. Gently press half of red dough evenly over plain dough. Repeat layers with remaining dough. Cover with the plastic wrap; refrigerate 2 hours or until firm.

3. Preheat oven to 350°. Remove dough from loaf pan; unwrap. Cut dough in half lengthwise. Cut each half crosswise into ¼-inch-thick slices. Place slices 2 inches apart on ungreased baking sheets. Bake at 350° 10 to 12 minutes or until set. Cool 2 minutes; remove from baking sheets to wire racks to cool completely.

color wow!

To make checkerboard cookies, cut layered dough into quarters lengthwise. Stack slices to create a checkerboard pattern before cutting into ¼-inch-thick slices.

gift tag cookies

MAKES 20 SERVINGS   Hands-On Time: 50 min.   Total Time: 2 hours, 15 min.

These cookies make any gift extra special. Write the recipient's name on the cookie, or pen a short phrase such as "Congrats!" or "Happy Birthday!"

1 (17.5-oz.) pouch sugar cookie mix

⅓ cup butter, softened

1 Tbsp. all-purpose flour

1 large egg

1 cup ready-to-spread cream cheese
    or vanilla frosting

Assorted food coloring pastes

String or ribbon

1. In medium bowl, stir cookie mix, butter, flour, and egg until soft dough forms. Shape dough into a ball; flatten slightly. Wrap in plastic wrap. Refrigerate 1 hour or until firm.

2. Preheat oven to 375°. On lightly floured surface, roll dough to ¼-inch thickness. Cut with 3-inch gift tag-shaped cutter (or cut into 3- x 2-inch rectangles, and cut ½ inch diagonally off 2 corners of rectangle). Place cutouts about 2 inches apart on ungreased baking sheets.

3. Bake at 375° for 10 to 12 minutes or until edges are lightly browned. Cool 2 minutes; remove from baking sheets to wire racks, and cool completely (about 20 minutes). Use a bamboo skewer or chopstick to make a hole at narrow end of each gift tag cookie.

4. Place ⅓ cup frosting in each of 3 small bowls; tint each frosting desired color. Spoon each color frosting into separate small zip-top plastic freezer bags; seal bags. Cut off tiny corner of each bag. Twist bag above frosting; squeeze to pipe details on gift tags. String ribbon through holes in cookies.

birthday cake cookies

MAKES 24 SERVINGS   Hands-On Time: 1 hour   Total Time: 2 hours, 55 min.

1 (17.5-oz.) pouch sugar cookie mix

2 Tbsp. all-purpose flour

½ cup butter, softened

1 large egg

Pouches of cookie icing in desired colors

¼ cup rainbow candy sprinkles

Sanding sugar in desired colors

1. In medium bowl, stir cookie mix, flour, butter, and egg until soft dough forms. Shape dough into a ball; flatten slightly. Wrap dough in plastic wrap; refrigerate 1 hour or until firm.

2. Preheat oven to 375°. On lightly floured surface, roll dough to ¼-inch thickness. Cut with a 3-inch cake-shaped cutter. Place cutouts 2 inches apart on ungreased baking sheets.

3. Bake at 375° for 8 to 10 minutes or until edges are lightly browned. Cool 5 minutes; remove from baking sheets to wire racks. Cool completely (about 20 minutes). Decorate cookies with icings, candy sprinkles, and sanding sugars. Let stand until set.

color wow!

Turn these cookies into bridal shower treats by using white icing and white sanding sugar with just a touch of color to accent.

under-the-sea cookies

Perfect for a pool party or beach vacation, these bubbly fish are a bright and cheerful way to welcome summer.

1 (17.5-oz.) pouch peanut butter cookie mix

2 Tbsp. all-purpose flour

3 Tbsp. vegetable oil

1 large egg

Pouches of cookie icing in desired colors

Orange, blue, green, and white sanding sugars

Candy eyes (optional)

1. In medium bowl, stir cookie mix, flour, oil, 1 Tbsp. water, and egg until soft dough forms. Shape dough into a ball; flatten slightly. Wrap dough in plastic wrap; refrigerate 1 hour or until firm.

2. Preheat oven to 350°. On lightly floured surface, roll dough to ¼-inch thickness. Cut with 3½-inch fish- and starfish-shaped cutters. Place cutouts 2 inches apart on ungreased baking sheets.

3. Bake at 350° for 9 to 11 minutes or until edges are lightly browned. Cool 5 minutes; remove from baking sheets to wire racks. Cool completely (about 20 minutes). Decorate cookies with icings and sugars. Attach candy eyes, if desired. Let stand until set.

simply smart

You can make these cookies with plain sugar cookie mix as an alternative to peanut butter cookie mix.

triple citrus layered cookies

MAKES 24 SERVINGS Hands-On Time: 20 min. Total Time: 2 hours, 5 min.

Love citrus but can't decide if you want lemon, lime, or orange? Not to worry—you can have all three in just one bite!

1 (18-oz.) package refrigerated sugar
   cookie dough
2 Tbsp. all-purpose flour
1 tsp. orange zest
Dash orange food coloring paste
1 tsp. lemon zest
Dash golden yellow food coloring
   paste
1 tsp. lime zest
Dash leaf green food coloring paste
1⅓ cups powdered sugar
5 tsp. fresh lemon juice
2 Tbsp. orange, green, and yellow
   sprinkles

1. Knead cookie dough and flour until blended. Divide dough into 3 equal portions.

2. Add orange zest and orange food coloring to 1 dough portion, kneading until combined. Add lemon zest and yellow food coloring to 1 dough portion, kneading until combined. Add lime zest and green food coloring to remaining dough portion, kneading until combined. Roll each dough portion into a 7- x 2-inch rectangle on a lightly floured surface. (Dough should be about ½ inch thick).

3. Stack doughs with orange dough on the bottom; top with green dough and yellow dough. Gently press doughs together. Wrap in plastic wrap, and freeze 1 hour.

4. Preheat oven to 350°. Unwrap dough, and cut into ¼-inch-thick slices. Place slices on ungreased baking sheets.

5. Bake cookies, in batches, at 350° for 8 to 10 minutes or until set. Cool on baking sheets 2 minutes. Transfer to wire racks, and cool completely (about 20 minutes).

6. Meanwhile, whisk together powdered sugar and lemon juice in a small bowl until smooth. Dip 1 edge of cookie into glaze; top with sprinkles. Place cookies on wax paper, and let stand until glaze is set (about 15 minutes).

clover cookies

MAKES 14 SERVINGS   Hands-On Time: 50 min.   Total Time: 2 hours, 45 min.

Nothing says "lucky" like shamrocks and four-leaf clovers! Serve these any time as a springtime treat, or impress your guests at a St. Patrick's Day party.

1 (17.5-oz.) pouch chocolate chunk cookie mix

¼ cup vegetable oil

1 large egg

1 (12-oz.) container whipped ready-to-spread white frosting

¼ tsp. Kelly green food coloring paste

⅛ tsp. lime green food coloring paste

Green and white sanding sugars

Green candy sprinkles

1. Process cookie mix in a food processor 10 seconds or until chocolate chunks are finely chopped. Add oil and egg; pulse until dough forms. Chill 1 hour.

2. Preheat oven to 350°. On lightly floured surface, roll dough to ¼-inch thickness. Cut with 3-inch clover- and shamrock-shaped cutters. Place cutouts 2 inches apart on ungreased baking sheets.

3. Bake at 350° for 8 to 10 minutes or until set. Cool 5 minutes; remove from baking sheets to wire racks. Cool completely (about 20 minutes).

4. Divide frosting between 2 small bowls; tint 1 bowl with Kelly green food coloring and 1 bowl with lime green food coloring. Frost half of cookies with each color. Spoon remaining frosting into separate zip-top plastic freezer bags; cut off one tiny corner of bags. Decorate cookies as desired with icing, sanding sugars, and sprinkles. Let stand until set.

butterfly cookies

MAKES 18 SERVINGS   Hands-On Time: 50 min.   Total Time: 2 hours, 45 min.

Watch as these beauties "fly" off the plate! Ice them all the same, or give each butterfly a unique look.

1 (17.5-oz.) pouch sugar cookie mix

2 Tbsp. all-purpose flour

½ cup butter, softened

1 large egg

1 (4.25-oz.) tube pink decorating icing

1 (4.25-oz.) tube purple decorating icing

1 (7-oz.) pouch white cookie icing

1 (7-oz.) pouch yellow cookie icing

Sanding sugars in desired colors

Additional candy sprinkles (optional)

1. In large bowl, stir cookie mix, flour, butter, and egg until soft dough forms. Shape dough into a ball; flatten slightly. Wrap dough in plastic wrap; refrigerate 1 hour or until firm.

2. Preheat oven to 375°. On lightly floured surface, roll dough to ¼-inch thickness. Cut with 3-inch butterfly-shaped cutters. Place cutouts 2 inches apart on ungreased baking sheets.

3. Bake at 375° for 12 to 13 minutes or until edges are golden brown. Cool 5 minutes; remove from baking sheets to wire racks. Cool completely (about 20 minutes). Decorate cookies with icings, sanding sugars, and candy sprinkles, if desired. Let stand until set.

color wow!

Make these cookies extra fun and colorful by adding 2 Tbsp. rainbow candy sprinkles to cookie dough. Continue with recipe as directed.

blue velvet pinwheel cookies

MAKES 28 SERVINGS   Hands-On Time: 35 min.   Total Time: 2 hours, 35 min.

1 (17.5-oz.) pouch sugar cookie mix

¼ cup butter, softened

1 (3-oz.) package cream cheese, softened

1 large egg

3 Tbsp. all-purpose flour

¼ tsp. blue food coloring gel

Wax paper

White sanding sugar

1. In large bowl, stir cookie mix, butter, cream cheese, and egg with spoon until soft dough forms. Divide dough in half. Add flour and food coloring to one half; mix until well blended and uniform in color.

2. Place blue dough between 2 (17- x 12-inch) sheets of wax paper; roll out to 12- x 7-inch rectangle. Repeat with plain dough; remove top sheet of wax paper from both doughs. Invert plain dough onto blue dough. Gently press out layered dough, and trim edges. Remove top sheet of wax paper from plain dough. Starting with short side, roll up dough, jelly-roll fashion, in bottom sheet of wax paper. Roll log in sanding sugar. Wrap tightly; freeze 2 hours or until very firm.

3. Preheat oven to 350°. Unwrap dough; cut into ¼-inch-thick slices. Place slices 2 inches apart on ungreased baking sheets. Bake at 350° for 12 to 15 minutes or until set. Cool 2 minutes; remove from baking sheets to wire racks, and cool completely (about 20 minutes).

color wow!

Turn these whirly cookies into red velvet pinwheels by substituting 2 Tbsp. unsweetened cocoa for the flour and ½ tsp. red food coloring gel for blue.

gingered peach pastries

MAKES 9 SERVINGS   Hands-On Time: 12 min.   Total Time: 57 min.

1 (11-oz.) package piecrust mix

⅓ cup cold water

Parchment paper

½ cup peach preserves

2 Tbsp. dark brown sugar

2 tsp. finely chopped crystallized ginger

¼ tsp. ground cinnamon

1 cup powdered sugar

4 tsp. milk

Peach food coloring gel

1. Preheat oven to 425°. Prepare piecrust mix according to package directions using cold water method.

2. Divide dough in half, and roll each dough portion into a 12- x 9-inch rectangle on a lightly floured surface. Cut each half of dough into 9 (4- x 3-inch) rectangles. Arrange rectangles on a large parchment paper-lined baking sheet.

3. Combine peach preserves, brown sugar, ginger, and cinnamon in a small bowl. Spoon about 1 Tbsp. peach filling down center of 9 dough rectangles to within ¾ inch of edges. Brush edges with cold water; top with remaining dough rectangles. Press edges together with a fork to seal. Freeze 10 minutes.

4. Bake at 425° for 20 minutes or until golden brown. Transfer to wire racks, and cool slightly, about 10 minutes.

5. Meanwhile, combine powdered sugar and milk, whisking until smooth. Set aside 3 Tbsp. glaze; tint remaining glaze with peach food coloring gel.

6. Spread white glaze over tops of pastries; drizzle with peach glaze, or decorate as desired.

color wow!

For added flair, cut out pastries in fun shapes, and let the kids do the decorating!

brilliant
bars

berry nerdy cereal bars

MAKES 16 SERVINGS   Hands-On Time: 20 min.   Total Time: 1 hour, 20 min.

Just when you thought marshmallow cereal bars couldn't get any better, along come Berry Nerdy Cereal Bars! Berry-flavored cereal is studded with tangy candies and held together with marshmallows and white chocolate. Oh yes—it just keeps getting better!

¼ cup butter

1 (10.5-oz.) bag miniature marshmallows

1½ cups white chocolate morsels, divided

8 cups berry-flavored sweetened corn-and-oat cereal

1 (5-oz.) package tiny, tangy, crunchy candy, divided

Cooking spray

1. Melt butter in a large saucepan over medium heat; add marshmallows and 1 cup morsels. Cook, stirring constantly, 2 minutes or until melted and smooth. Remove from heat.

2. Stir in cereal and ½ cup crunchy candy until well coated.

3. Using wet or lightly greased hands, press mixture into a 13- x 9-inch pan coated with cooking spray.

4. Microwave remaining ½ cup morsels in a small microwave-safe bowl at HIGH 1 minute or until melted and smooth, stirring at 20-second intervals. Drizzle chocolate over bars in pan. Sprinkle with remaining 2 Tbsp. crunchy candy. Chill 1 hour. Cut into 16 bars.

Note: We tested with Wonka Rainbow NERDS® for tiny, tangy, crunchy candy and Cap'n Crunch® Oops! All Berries for berry-flavored sweetened corn-and-oat cereal.

cheery chocolate candy bars

MAKES 16 SERVINGS   Hands-On Time: 25 min.   Total Time: 2 hours, 22 min.

Use any variety of candy-coated chocolate candy for this colorful cookie treat.

1 (17.5-oz.) pouch sugar cookie mix

2 Tbsp. all-purpose flour

Lemon yellow food coloring paste

6 Tbsp. butter, softened

3 cups powdered sugar

1/3 cup unsweetened cocoa

1/4 cup whipping cream

1½ tsp. vanilla extract

1 cup orange candy melts

1/2 cup yellow candy melts

3/4 cup candy-coated chocolate
    pieces

1. Preheat oven to 350°. Line the bottom and sides of a 9-inch square pan with aluminum foil, allowing 2 to 3 inches to extend over sides; lightly grease foil.

2. Prepare cookie dough according to package directions for cutout cookies, adding flour and tinting light yellow with food coloring. Press mixture evenly into prepared pan.

3. Bake at 350° for 20 minutes or until golden brown and set. Cool completely in pan on a wire rack (about 1 hour).

4. Beat butter at medium speed with an electric mixer until creamy. Combine powdered sugar and cocoa; gradually add to butter alternately with cream, beating at low speed until well blended after each addition. Beat in vanilla. Beat at medium speed 30 seconds or until light and fluffy. Spread frosting over cooled bars in pan. Chill 30 minutes.

5. In two separate microwave-safe bowls, microwave candy melts at MEDIUM for 2 minutes, stirring every 15 seconds until melted and smooth. Spread orange melted candy over chocolate frosting. Drizzle with yellow melted candy, and swirl with a toothpick. Sprinkle with chocolate pieces. Let stand 10 minutes or until set. Lift bars from pan, using foil sides as handles. Gently remove foil, and cut into 16 bars.

neapolitan bars

MAKES 20 SERVINGS Hands-On Time: 17 min. Total Time: 47 min.

. . . .

Enjoy the classic Neapolitan flavors of strawberry, chocolate, and vanilla in a fun new way with these rice cereal bars

2 oz. bittersweet chocolate, chopped

6 Tbsp. butter, divided

1 (16-oz.) bag miniature
    marshmallows, divided

4 cups chocolate-flavored crisp rice
    cereal

Cooking spray

8 cups crisp rice cereal, divided

1 (8-oz.) bag strawberry-flavored
    marshmallows

1 Tbsp. each chocolate, white, and
    pink jimmies

1. Microwave chocolate and 2 Tbsp. butter in a large microwave-safe glass bowl at HIGH for 45 seconds or until melted and smooth, stirring after 30 seconds.

2. Stir in 4½ cups miniature marshmallows. Microwave at HIGH 1 to 1½ minutes or until puffed and melted. Immediately stir in chocolate-flavored crisp rice cereal until well coated. Using wet or lightly greased hands, press mixture into a 13- x 9-inch pan coated with cooking spray.

3. Microwave 2 Tbsp. butter and remaining 4½ cups miniature marshmallows in a separate large microwave-safe glass bowl at HIGH 1 to 1½ minutes or until puffed and melted. Immediately stir in 4 cups crisp rice cereal until well coated. Using wet or lightly greased hands, press mixture evenly on top of chocolate layer in pan.

4. Microwave remaining 2 Tbsp. butter and strawberry-flavored marshmallows in a separate large microwave-safe glass bowl at HIGH 1 to 1½ minutes or until puffed and melted. Immediately stir in remaining 4 cups crisp rice cereal until well coated. Using wet or lightly greased hands, press mixture evenly on top of white layer in pan. Sprinkle with jimmies. Let stand 30 minutes or until firm. Cut into 20 bars.

italian rainbow bars

MAKES 32 SERVINGS   Hands-On Time: 25 min.   Total Time: 2 hours, 35 min.

The classic in colorful bars, these dense almond and raspberry treats are just like Nonna used to make!

Cooking spray
Parchment paper
2 cups all-purpose flour
¼ tsp. baking powder
¼ tsp. table salt
1¼ cups butter, softened
1 cup sugar
1 (7-oz.) package marzipan (almond paste), crumbled
½ tsp. almond extract
3 large eggs
¼ tsp. green food coloring paste
½ tsp. red food coloring paste
⅓ cup seedless raspberry jam
8 oz. bittersweet baking chocolate, chopped
¼ cup whipping cream

1. Preheat oven to 350°. Spray a 13- x 9-inch pan with cooking spray; line with parchment paper, allowing 1 inch of paper to extend over sides. Spray paper with cooking spray.

2. Whisk together flour, baking powder, and salt. In medium bowl, beat butter, sugar, marzipan, and almond extract at medium speed with an electric mixer 5 minutes or until light and fluffy. Beat in eggs, 1 at a time, until blended. On low speed, gradually beat in flour mixture.

3. Spread one-third of the batter (1½ cups) evenly in prepared pan (layer will be very thin). Freeze 5 minutes.

4. Meanwhile, in small bowl, mix green food coloring into one-third (1½ cups) of the batter. Gently spread over batter in pan. Freeze 5 minutes. In separate small bowl, mix red food coloring into remaining batter. Gently spread over green batter.

5. Bake at 350° for 24 to 28 minutes or until a wooden pick inserted in center comes out clean. Cool completely in pan on a wire rack, about 1 hour. Spread jam over bars. In microwave-safe bowl, microwave chocolate and whipping cream at HIGH about 1 minute, stirring once or until mixture is smooth. Spread chocolate mixture over jam. Refrigerate 30 minutes or until chocolate is set. Use paper to lift out of pan. Gently remove paper. Trim edges, if desired. Cut into 8 rows by 4 rows. Store loosely covered.

raspberry-lemon
squares

MAKES 9 SERVINGS   Hands-On Time: 35 min.   Total Time: 4 hours, 30 min.

A cool and refreshing twist on the lemon bar, these raspberry-packed treats have a surprise layer of cream cheese!

Cooking spray

½ (16-oz.) package refrigerated ready-to-bake sugar cookie dough

2 cups fresh raspberries

1½ cups granulated sugar

2 Tbsp. lemon zest

½ cup fresh lemon juice (about 4 lemons)

1 large egg

4 large egg whites

⅛ tsp. table salt

⅓ cup all-purpose flour

¾ cup cream cheese spread (from 8-oz container)

1 cup whipping cream

2 Tbsp. powdered sugar

1 cup fresh raspberries

Garnish: lemon rind twists

1. Preheat oven to 350°. Line bottom and sides of an 8- or 9-inch square pan with aluminum foil, allowing 1 inch to extend over sides; spray foil with cooking spray.

2. Press dough evenly on bottom of pan. Bake at 350° for 20 to 25 minutes or until light golden brown. Cool completely in pan on a wire rack.

3. Meanwhile, in food processor, place 2 cups raspberries. Cover; process until smooth. Strain raspberries through a strainer into a medium bowl to remove seeds. Add granulated sugar, lemon zest, lemon juice, egg, egg whites, and salt; mix well. Stir in flour with whisk just until blended. Spread cream cheese spread over cooled cookie crust. Pour raspberry filling over cream cheese layer.

4. Bake 50 to 55 minutes or until filling is set. Cool completely in pan on wire rack. Cover; refrigerate at least 2 hours. Lift from pan, using foil sides as handles. Gently remove foil. Cut into 3 rows by 3 rows.

5. In chilled medium bowl, beat whipping cream and powdered sugar at high speed with an electric mixer until soft peaks form. Top squares with whipped cream and 1 cup raspberries.

key lime bars

MAKES 24 SERVINGS   Hands-On Time: 10 min.   Total Time: 2 hours, 52 min.

A sweet, buttery macadamia shortbread crust adds to the island flavor of a tangy Key lime custard.

Cooking spray
2 cups all-purpose flour
2/3 cup macadamia nuts
1/2 cup powdered sugar
1 cup cold butter, cut into pieces
1 3/4 cups granulated sugar
1/4 cup cornstarch
3 large eggs
3 large egg yolks
1 Tbsp. lime zest
3/4 cup bottled Key lime juice
4 drops green liquid food coloring
Powdered sugar

1. Preheat oven to 350°. Line the bottom and sides of a 13- x 9-inch pan with aluminum foil, allowing 2 to 3 inches to extend over sides; coat heavily with cooking spray.

2. Pulse flour, nuts, and 1/2 cup powdered sugar in a food processor 20 seconds or until nuts are finely ground. Add butter; pulse 15 times or until crumbly. Press dough on bottom and 1 inch up sides of prepared pan.

3. Bake at 350° for 20 minutes or until lightly browned.

4. Whisk together granulated sugar and cornstarch in a medium bowl. Whisk in eggs and egg yolks. Whisk in lime zest, Key lime juice, and food coloring. Pour mixture over crust.

5. Bake at 350° for 22 minutes or until set. Cool completely in pan on a wire rack (about 2 hours). Lift from pan, using foil sides as handles. Gently remove foil, and sprinkle with powdered sugar. Cut into 24 bars, or use a round biscuit cutter to cut into rounds.

pink lemonade
bars

MAKES 24 SERVINGS   Hands-On Time: 11 min.   Total Time: 3 hours, 45 min.

1 (17.5-oz.) pouch sugar cookie mix

⅓ cup butter, softened

5 large eggs, divided

¼ cup plus 1 Tbsp. all-purpose flour, divided

1½ cups granulated sugar

⅛ tsp. table salt

½ cup fresh lemon juice (about 4 lemons)

2 Tbsp. grenadine

Powdered sugar

1. Preheat oven to 350°. Line the bottom and sides of a 13- x 9-inch pan with aluminum foil, allowing 2 to 3 inches to extend over sides; lightly grease foil.

2. Stir sugar cookie mix, butter, 1 egg, and 1 Tbsp. flour with a wooden spoon until dough forms. Press dough on bottom and ½ inch up sides of prepared pan. Bake at 350° for 12 minutes or until edges are light golden brown. Cool completely in pan on a wire rack (about 1 hour).

3. Whisk together granulated sugar, salt, and the remaining ¼ cup flour in a large bowl. Add remaining 4 eggs; whisk until smooth. Add lemon juice and grenadine, and stir until combined. Pour mixture over cooled crust.

4. Bake at 350° for 22 minutes or until center is set. Cool completely in pan on a wire rack (about 2 hours). Lift from pan, using foil sides as handles. Gently remove foil, and cut into 24 bars. Sprinkle with powdered sugar just before serving.

color wow!

These tangy bars bake up in a soft shade of pink. If you want a bolder look, add ¼ tsp. red food coloring paste with the grenadine.

cherry squares

MAKES 16 SERVINGS   Hands-On Time: 17 min.   Total Time: 3 hours, 2 min.

Top these cherry-flavored blondies with bright red Bing cherries or tart Montmorency cherries for the best pop of color.

1½ cups all-purpose flour
1 tsp. baking powder
¼ tsp. table salt
1¼ cups sugar
¾ cup butter, melted
1 large egg
1 large egg yolk
1 tsp. vanilla extract
¼ cup cherry preserves
1½ Tbsp. cherry liqueur, divided
½ cup whipping cream
Disposable decorating bag
16 fresh cherries

1. Preheat oven to 350°. Line the bottom and sides of an 8-inch square pan with aluminum foil, allowing 2 to 3 inches to extend over sides; lightly grease foil.

2. Combine flour, baking powder, and salt in a small bowl. Whisk together sugar, butter, egg, egg yolk, and vanilla in a large bowl. Add flour mixture to butter mixture, and stir until combined. Pour half of batter into prepared pan; freeze 10 minutes or until firm.

3. Add preserves and 1 Tbsp. cherry liqueur to remaining batter; pour over batter in pan. Bake at 350° for 35 minutes or until a wooden pick inserted in center comes out clean. Cool completely in pan on a wire rack (about 2 hours). Lift from pan, using foil sides as handles. Gently remove foil, and cut into 16 squares.

4. Beat whipping cream and remaining ½ Tbsp. cherry liqueur at high speed with an electric mixer until stiff peaks form. Spoon whipped cream into a disposable decorating bag fitted with a star tip; pipe onto bars. Top each bar with a cherry.

tropical sunset bars

MAKES 16 SERVINGS   Hands-On Time: 10 min.   Total Time: 2 hours, 10 min.

These no-bake bars are just like a piña colada, with juicy pineapple and a creamy coconut cheesecake.

1 (11.1-oz.) package no-bake
    cheesecake mix
2 Tbsp. sugar
6 Tbsp. butter, melted
1 (20-oz.) can crushed pineapple
    in syrup, drained
3 Tbsp. coconut-flavored rum
1½ cups milk
⅛ tsp. yellow food coloring paste
½ tsp. orange food coloring paste
1⅓ cups sweetened shredded
    coconut, toasted

1. Prepare cheesecake crust according to package directions, adding 2 Tbsp. sugar and using 6 Tbsp butter; press mixture onto the bottom of a lightly greased 8-inch square pan. Combine pineapple and rum; spread over crust.

2. Prepare cheesecake filling according to package directions, using milk and adding yellow food coloring. Pour batter into pan over pineapple.

3. Dip end of a wooden pick into orange food coloring, and swirl through batter; swirl batter with a knife. Press coconut on top, and chill until set (about 2 hours). Cut into 16 bars.

blackberry
cheesecake bites

MAKES 36 SERVINGS   Hands-On Time: 25 min.   Total Time: 4 hours, 35 min.

These party-perfect cheesecakes pack rich, creamy decadence into a single bite!

Cooking spray

15 graham cracker squares

½ cup sliced almonds

1¼ cups sugar, divided

⅓ cup butter, melted

3 (8-oz.) packages cream cheese, softened

2 Tbsp. all-purpose flour

1 tsp. vanilla extract

3 large eggs

⅓ cup seedless blackberry jam

36 fresh blackberries

Fresh mint leaves (optional)

1. Preheat oven to 350°. Line bottom and sides of a 9-inch square pan with aluminum foil, allowing 1 inch to extend over sides; spray foil with cooking spray. Pulse crackers, almonds, and ¼ cup sugar in a food processor until finely ground. Add melted butter. Cover; process until mixture looks like wet sand. Press onto bottom of pan.

2. Bake at 350° for 10 to 12 minutes or until golden brown. Cool completely in pan on a wire rack. Meanwhile, in large bowl, beat cream cheese, remaining 1 cup sugar, flour, and vanilla at medium speed with an electric mixer until smooth. On low speed, beat in eggs, 1 at a time, just until blended after each addition. Pour filling over crust.

3. Spoon small dollops of jam over filling; swirl with knife. Bake at 350° for 35 to 40 minutes or until set. Cool in pan on wire rack 1 hour. Cover and refrigerate 2 hours. Lift from pan, using foil sides as handles; gently remove foil. Cut into 36 squares. Top each cheesecake bite with 1 blackberry and, if desired, mint leaf. Store covered in refrigerator.

pistachio cream bars

MAKES 24 SERVINGS   Hands-On Time: 30 min.   Total Time: 4 hours, 10 min.

Whip up these bars for a light-as-air dessert with a pistachio crunch

Cooking spray
1 cup butter, softened
2/3 cup powdered sugar
2 cups all-purpose flour
1/4 tsp. baking powder
1/2 cup finely chopped pistachios
1 1/2 cups whipping cream
2 (8-oz.) packages cream cheese,
    softened
1 cup powdered sugar
1/2 tsp. vanilla extract
1 (3.4-oz.) package pistachio
    instant pudding
1 cup milk
Garnish: chopped pistachios

1. Preheat oven to 350°. Spray bottom and sides of a 13- x 9-inch pan with cooking spray.

2. In large bowl, beat butter and 2/3 cup powdered sugar at low speed with an electric mixer until blended. Beat at medium speed until light and fluffy. Gradually add flour and baking powder, beating until blended. Stir in 1/2 cup nuts. Press dough onto bottom of pan.

3. Bake at 350° for 30 to 35 minutes or until golden brown. Cool completely in pan on a wire rack (about 1 hour).

4. In chilled medium bowl, beat whipping cream at high speed with mixer until soft peaks form. In another medium bowl, beat cream cheese and 1 cup powdered sugar at medium speed 1 minute or until creamy. Fold in vanilla and 1 1/2 cups of the whipped cream. Spread over baked crust. Keep refrigerated.

5. In medium bowl, mix pudding mix and 1 cup milk according to package directions. Refrigerate 5 minutes. Fold in remaining whipped cream. Spread over cream cheese layer. Refrigerate at least 2 hours or until set. Cut into 24 bars. Store covered in refrigerator.

raspberry swirl
cheesecake bars

MAKES 20 SERVINGS   Hands-On Time: 15 min.   Total Time: 2 hours, 10 min.

Cooking spray

24 thin chocolate wafer cookies,
    crushed (1½ cups crumbs)

6 Tbsp. butter, melted

2 (8-oz.) packages cream cheese,
    softened

½ cup sugar

2 large eggs

2 Tbsp. all-purpose flour

½ tsp. almond extract

⅓ cup seedless red raspberry jam

20 fresh raspberries

1. Preheat oven to 325°. Line bottom and sides of an 8-inch square pan with aluminum foil, allowing 1 inch to extend over sides of pan; spray foil with cooking spray.

2. In medium bowl, mix cookie crumbs and butter. Press into pan. Bake at 325° for 12 minutes. Cool 15 minutes.

3. Meanwhile, in another medium bowl, beat cream cheese and sugar at medium speed with an electric mixer until smooth. Add eggs, 1 at a time, beating just until blended after each addition. Add flour and almond extract, beating just until blended. Pour over cooled crust. Drop jam by teaspoonfuls over batter; swirl jam through batter with knife for marbled design.

4. Bake at 325° for 30 to 40 minutes or until set. Cool completely in pan on wire rack (about 1 hour). Lift from pan, using foil sides as handles; gently remove foil. Cut into 20 bars; top each bar with 1 raspberry. Store in refrigerator.

Note: We tested with Nabisco Famous Chocolate Wafers.

polka-dot
cheesecake brownies

MAKES 18 SERVINGS   Hands-On Time: 30 min.   Total Time: 4 hours, 40 min.

Cooking spray

1 (17-oz.) package dark chocolate
　　brownie mix

Water, vegetable oil, and eggs called
　　for on brownie mix box

4 (8-oz.) packages cream cheese,
　　softened

1 cup sugar

1 tsp. vanilla extract

¼ cup all-purpose flour

4 large eggs

2 Tbsp. seedless strawberry jam

¼ tsp. red food coloring paste

2 oz. semisweet baking chocolate,
　　melted and cooled

1. Preheat oven to 350°. Line bottom and sides of a 13- x 9-inch pan with aluminum foil, allowing 1 inch to extend over sides; spray foil with cooking spray. Prepare brownie mix according to package directions, using water, oil, and eggs.

2. Bake at 350° for 15 minutes; cool 15 minutes. Reduce oven temperature to 325°. In large bowl, beat cream cheese, sugar, and vanilla at medium speed with an electric mixer until well blended. Beat in flour. Beat in eggs, 1 at a time, until blended.

3. In small bowl, mix 1 cup cheesecake batter, jam, and food coloring. In another bowl, mix 1 cup cheesecake batter and melted chocolate. Gently spoon remaining cheesecake batter over warm brownie layer. Spoon strawberry batter into a zip-top plastic freezer bag. Seal bag; cut off small corner of bag. Squeeze to pipe dots over surface of cheesecake batter. Repeat with chocolate batter.

4. Bake at 325° for 35 to 40 minutes or until set. Cool in pan on wire rack 1 hour. Refrigerate 2 hours. Lift from pan, using foil sides as handles. Gently remove foil. Cut into 18 bars.

orange cream swirl bars

MAKES 24 SERVINGS   Hands-On Time: 15 min.   Total Time: 1 hour, 45 min.

1 (4-oz.) white chocolate baking bar, chopped

¾ cup butter

1¾ cups sugar, divided

4 large eggs

2 tsp. orange zest

2 tsp. vanilla extract, divided

½ tsp. orange food coloring paste

1½ cups plus 1 Tbsp. all-purpose flour, divided

⅛ tsp. table salt

1 (8-oz.) package cream cheese, softened

1 large egg yolk

1. Preheat oven to 350°. Microwave white chocolate and butter in a large microwave-safe bowl at HIGH 1 to 1½ minutes or until melted and smooth, stirring at 30-second intervals. Whisk in 1½ cups sugar. Add eggs, 1 at a time, whisking just until blended after each addition. Add orange zest, 1 tsp. vanilla, and food coloring. Gently stir in 1½ cups flour and salt. Spread batter into a greased 13- x 9-inch pan.

2. Beat cream cheese and remaining ¼ cup sugar at medium speed with an electric mixer until fluffy. Add egg yolk and remaining 1 tsp. vanilla; beat until blended. Beat in remaining 1 Tbsp. flour until smooth. Dollop cream cheese mixture over orange batter in pan; gently swirl with a knife.

3. Bake at 350° for 28 to 30 minutes or until a wooden pick inserted in center comes out with a few moist crumbs. Cool completely in pan on a wire rack (about 1 hour). Cut into 24 squares.

birthday blondies

1 (16.5-oz.) package yellow cake mix
6 Tbsp. canola oil
1 large egg
⅓ cup milk
¼ tsp. almond extract
½ cup toasted slivered almonds
¼ cup plus 2 Tbsp. rainbow candy or
    confetti sprinkles, divided

1. Preheat oven to 350°. Lightly grease a 9-inch square pan.

2. Stir together first 5 ingredients in a large bowl (batter will be thick). Stir in almonds and ¼ cup sprinkles. Spread batter into prepared pan. Sprinkle with remaining 2 Tbsp. sprinkles.

3. Bake at 350° for 23 to 25 minutes or until set and lightly browned. Cool completely in pan on a wire rack (about 1 hour). Cut into 16 squares.

simply smart

Although it might seem as though there could never be too many sprinkles, don't add more to the batter than called for, or they will muddle together into a murky hue.

peanut butter cup brownie bars

MAKES 24 SERVINGS   Hands-On Time: 15 min.   Total Time: 3 hours

Peanut butter and chocolate make a classic combination in these spin-offs of 7-Layer Bars topped with lots of peanut butter candy.

1 (19.5-oz.) package chocolate fudge brownie mix
1 (14-oz.) can sweetened condensed milk
1 cup lightly salted roasted peanuts
½ cup peanut butter morsels
½ cup semisweet chocolate morsels
1 cup candy-coated peanut butter pieces
15 miniature peanut butter cup candies, unwrapped and quartered and divided (1 cup)

1. Preheat oven to 350°. Line the bottom and sides of a 13- x 9-inch pan with aluminum foil, allowing 2 inches to extend over sides; lightly grease foil.

2. Prepare brownie batter according to package directions. Spread batter into prepared pan. Bake at 350° for 20 minutes or until a wooden pick inserted into center comes out clean.

3. Remove brownies from oven. Top evenly with sweetened condensed milk, peanuts, morsels, peanut butter pieces, and ½ cup peanut butter cup candies; bake 20 to 25 more minutes or until mixture is bubbly and edges are golden brown.

4. Remove from oven; top with remaining ½ cup peanut butter cup candies. Cool completely in pan on a wire rack (about 2 hours). Lift from pan, using foil sides as handles. Gently remove foil, and cut into 24 bars.

red velvet brownies

MAKES 16 SERVINGS

Hands-On Time: 15 min.   Total Time: 3 hours, 10 min., including frosting

1 (4-oz.) bittersweet chocolate baking bar, chopped
¾ cup butter
2 cups sugar
4 large eggs
1½ cups all-purpose flour
1 (1-oz.) bottle red liquid food coloring
1½ tsp. baking powder
1 tsp. vanilla extract
⅛ tsp. table salt
Small-Batch Cream Cheese Frosting
Garnish: white chocolate curls

small-batch cream cheese frosting

Beat 1 (8-oz.) package softened cream cheese and 3 Tbsp. softened butter at medium speed with an electric mixer until creamy. Gradually add 1½ cups powdered sugar and ⅛ tsp. table salt, beating until blended. Stir in 1 tsp. vanilla extract. Makes about 1⅔ cups.

1. Preheat oven to 350°. Line the bottom and sides of a 9-inch square pan with aluminum foil, allowing 2 to 3 inches to extend over sides; lightly grease foil.

2. Microwave chocolate and butter in a large microwave-safe bowl at HIGH 1½ to 2 minutes or until melted and smooth, stirring at 30-second intervals. Whisk in sugar. Add eggs, 1 at a time, whisking just until blended after each addition. Gently stir in flour and next 4 ingredients. Pour mixture into prepared pan.

3. Bake at 350° for 44 to 48 minutes or until a wooden pick inserted in center comes out with a few moist crumbs. Cool completely in pan on a wire rack (about 2 hours).

4. Lift from pan, using foil sides as handles; gently remove foil. Spread frosting on top of brownies, and cut into 16 squares.

mint chocolate brownies

MAKES 16 SERVINGS   Hands-On Time: 30 min.   Total Time: 2 hours

1 (18.75-oz.) package brownie mix
½ cup butter, softened
1½ cups powdered sugar
1 Tbsp. milk
1 tsp. peppermint extract
6 drops green liquid food coloring
2 drops yellow liquid food coloring
Shaved thin crème de menthe
    chocolate mints

1. Preheat oven to 350°. Line the bottom and sides of an 8-inch square pan with aluminum foil, allowing 2 to 3 inches to extend over sides; lightly grease foil. Prepare brownie batter according to package directions; pour into prepared pan.

2. Bake at 350° according to package directions. Cool completely in pan on a wire rack (about 1 hour).

3. Meanwhile, beat butter and powdered sugar at medium-low speed with an electric mixer until combined; add milk, peppermint extract, and food colorings, beating until blended. Increase speed to medium-high, and beat 1 minute or until fluffy.

4. Lift brownies from pan, using foil sides as handles. Gently remove foil. Spread frosting evenly over brownies, and cut into 16 squares. Sprinkle with thinly shaved mints.

Note: We tested with Ghirardelli Chocolate Supreme Brownie Mix and Andes Crème de Menthe Thins.

simply smart

Use a vegetable peeler to create curls from the thin crème de menthe chocolate mints. If you have time, freeze the mints, as they tend to melt quickly as you are making the curls.

cool
treats

sunset ice pops

MAKES 10 SERVINGS   Hands-On Time: 12 min.   Total Time: 8 hours, 12 min.

1 (20-oz.) can pineapple chunks in syrup, undrained

10 (5-oz.) plastic cups or ice pop molds

¾ cup frozen orange juice concentrate, thawed

10 (4-inch) wooden craft sticks

1 cup cranberry juice cocktail

⅓ cup frozen limeade concentrate, thawed

simply smart

Ice pop molds come in many sizes; if yours are a different size, this recipe will still work but may give you a different amount of finished pops.

1. Process pineapple chunks and syrup in a blender or food processor until smooth. Press through a wire-mesh strainer using the back of a spoon to squeeze out 1 cup juice. Discard solids, and reserve remaining juice for another use. Pour mixture into plastic cups. Freeze 2 hours or until firm.

2. Whisk together orange juice concentrate and ½ cup water in a large glass measuring cup. Pour mixture over pineapple mixture in cups. Cover each cup with aluminum foil; insert a wooden stick into center of each pop. Freeze 2 hours or until firm.

3. Whisk together cranberry juice and limeade concentrate in a large glass measuring cup. Carefully remove foil from plastic cups, and pour cranberry juice mixture over orange layer. Freeze 4 hours or until firm.

frozen berry-yogurt
ice pops

MAKES 8 SERVINGS   Hands-On Time: 4 min.   Total Time: 4 hours, 9 min.

Vanilla yogurt and frozen fruit combine for a delicious
and healthy frozen treat.

2 cups vanilla yogurt

½ cup frozen blueberries

1 Tbsp. blueberry preserves

8 (4-oz.) ice pop molds

¼ cup blackberry jam

8 (4-inch) wooden craft sticks

1. Process 1 cup vanilla yogurt, blueberries, and blueberry preserves in a blender until smooth. Pour mixture into ice pop molds. Top with blackberry jam and remaining 1 cup vanilla yogurt, and swirl. Cover each mold with foil; insert a wooden stick into each pop. Freeze 4 hours or until pops are frozen.

2. Dip bottom of molds in warm water for a few seconds to release pops.

simply smart

If you want to make several batches of these pops but only have one set of molds, just freeze pops, remove from molds, and place in zip-top plastic freezer bags before returning to freezer. Wash molds before starting a second or third batch of pops.

tri-color fruit pops

MAKES 8 SERVINGS   Hands-On Time: 10 min.   Total Time: 4 hours, 40 min.

1½ cups lime sherbet

8 (5-oz.) ice pop molds or
    disposable plastic cups

1 cup pineapple sherbet

1½ cups raspberry sorbet

8 wooden craft sticks

1. Let lime sherbet stand at room temperature 20 minutes to soften, stirring occasionally. Spoon sherbet evenly into pop molds, and freeze 30 minutes or until slightly firm.

2. Let pineapple sherbet stand at room temperature 20 minutes to soften, stirring occasionally. Spoon over lime sherbet in pop molds, and freeze 1 hour or until slightly firm.

3. Let raspberry sorbet stand at room temperature 20 minutes to soften, stirring occasionally. Spoon sorbet over pineapple sherbet in pop molds. Insert a wooden stick into center of mixture. Freeze 2 hours or until sticks are solidly anchored and pops are completely frozen.

color wow!

Choose your favorite flavors of sherbet and sorbet for fruit pops of just about any color combination!

red, white, and blueberry pops

MAKES 10 SERVINGS   Hands-On Time: 30 min.   Total Time: 8 hours, 30 min.

1½ cups small fresh strawberries
    (12 small)
½ cup frozen (thawed) lemonade
    concentrate, divided
10 (4-oz.) ice pop molds
1¼ cups coconut sorbet, softened
10 (4-inch) wooden craft sticks
2 cups fresh blueberries

1. Process strawberries in a blender or food processor at medium speed 30 seconds or until smooth. Press through a small strainer into a medium bowl to remove seeds. Stir ¼ cup lemonade concentrate into strawberry puree. Divide mixture among ice pop molds. Freeze 2 hours or until firm.

2. Spoon 2 Tbsp. coconut sorbet evenly over strawberry layer in each ice pop. Cover each mold with foil; insert a wooden stick into each pop. Freeze 2 hours or until firm.

3. Process blueberries in a blender or food processor at medium speed 30 seconds or until smooth. Press through a small strainer into a medium bowl. Stir remaining ¼ cup lemonade concentrate into blueberry puree. Gently remove foil from each mold. Spoon mixture evenly over sorbet layer. Freeze at least 4 hours or overnight until firm.

simply smart

The warmth of your hand will help release the pops from the molds. Serve pops in trays of ice or standing up in a bucket of ice.

pineapple-mango-kiwi pops

MAKES 8 SERVINGS   Hands-On Time: 10 min.   Total Time: 9 hours, 10 min.

1 kiwifruit, peeled and cut into 8 slices

8 (3-oz.) ice pop molds

1 cup chopped fresh mango

¾ cup mango nectar

4 Tbsp. honey, divided

1 tsp. lime zest

¹⁄₁₆ tsp. orange food coloring paste

1 (8-oz.) can pineapple chunks in 100% pineapple juice, undrained

¾ cup pineapple juice

2 tsp. finely chopped crystallized ginger

8 (4-inch) wooden craft sticks

1. Place 1 kiwi slice into each ice pop mold.

2. Reserve ¼ cup chopped mango. Process the remaining ¾ cup mango, mango nectar, 2 Tbsp. honey, and lime zest in a blender until smooth. Stir in food coloring and reserved chopped mango. Pour mixture into molds (about 2 Tbsp. in each), and freeze until slightly firm, about 1 hour.

3. Meanwhile, chop pineapple chunks (reserve juice in can). Reserve ¼ cup chopped pineapple chunks. Process remaining pineapple chunks with juice in can, pineapple juice, ginger, and remaining 2 Tbsp. honey in a blender until smooth. Stir in reserved chopped pineapple chunks. Skim foam off top of mixture. Pour mixture into molds (about 3 Tbsp. in each). Insert craft sticks, and freeze 8 hours or until firm.

color wow!

Check your local crafts store for a variety of colored craft sticks to liven up these pops for a party.

watermelon margarita pops

MAKES 12 POPS   Hands-On Time: 15 min.   Total Time: 8 hours, 15 min.

6 limes

4 cups chopped seedless watermelon

¾ cup tequila

½ cup sugar

12 (3-oz.) paper cups

12 (3½-inch) decorative party picks
    or food-safe wooden ice-cream
    spoons

1. Grate zest from 1 lime to equal 1 tsp. Squeeze juice from limes to equal ½ cup. Process lime juice and watermelon in a blender until smooth. Pour through a fine wire-mesh strainer into a large measuring cup, discarding solids. Stir in tequila, sugar, and 1 tsp. lime zest, stirring until sugar dissolves. Pour mixture into paper cups.

2. Cover each cup with aluminum foil; make a small slit in center, and insert 1 party pick into each cup. Freeze 8 hours or until firm.

color wow!

Take these pops to the next level by sticking each party pick through a slice of lime before placing into mixture, omitting foil. Freeze as directed.

raspberry lemonade
pops

MAKES 10 SERVINGS   Hands-On Time: 15 min.   Total Time: 8 hours, 15 min.

Fresh raspberries peek out from a tart, lemony layer while a bright pink layer tops off these icy treats.

1 (12-oz.) can frozen lemonade
    concentrate

1 cup fresh raspberries, divided

½ cup plain yogurt, divided

10 (4-oz.) ice pop molds

10 (4-inch) wooden craft sticks

1. In a 1-qt. saucepan, heat lemonade concentrate and 1 cup water over medium heat just until lemonade concentrate is completely thawed; remove from heat, and cool. Process ¾ cup lemonade mixture, ½ cup raspberries, and ¼ cup yogurt in a blender at medium speed until smooth. Press mixture through a small strainer into a medium bowl to remove seeds.

2. Divide mixture evenly among ice pop molds. Freeze 4 hours or until firm.

3. Divide remaining ½ cup raspberries evenly among molds. In small bowl, mix 1 cup lemonade mixture and remaining ¼ cup yogurt. Divide evenly among molds. Cover each mold with foil; insert 1 wooden stick into each pop. Freeze 4 hours or until firm.

fizzy, fruity ice-cream floats

MAKES 6 SERVINGS Hands-On Time: 5 min. Total Time: 5 min.

A frosty dessert is never this easy. Guests can pick their favorite fruit-flavored soft drink and let the colorful creations flow.

4 cups vanilla ice cream
6 (12-oz.) fruit-flavored soft drinks, such as grape, orange, lime, or black cherry

1. Place 2 ($\frac{1}{3}$-cup) scoops of vanilla ice cream into each of 6 large glasses. Pour soft drinks over ice cream.

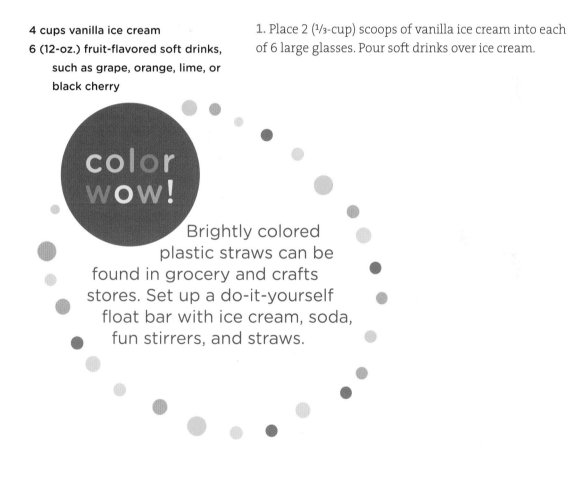

color wow!

Brightly colored plastic straws can be found in grocery and crafts stores. Set up a do-it-yourself float bar with ice cream, soda, fun stirrers, and straws.

rainbow
gellies

MAKES 8 SERVINGS Hands-On Time: 15 min. Total Time: 2 hours, 15 min.

8 (4-oz.) gelatin molds

1 (3-oz.) package strawberry-flavored
gelatin

2 cups boiling water, divided

2 cups cold water, divided

1 (3-oz.) package lemon-flavored
gelatin

1 (3-oz.) package lime-flavored
gelatin

1 (3-oz.) package berry blue-flavored
gelatin

1. Lightly grease gelatin molds.

2. Stir together strawberry gelatin and ½ cup boiling water 1 minute or until gelatin dissolves. Add ½ cup cold water; divide among prepared molds, and chill 30 minutes or until firm.

3. Stir together lemon gelatin and ½ cup boiling water 1 minute or until gelatin dissolves. Add ½ cup cold water; pour over strawberry gelatin in prepared molds, and chill 30 minutes or until firm.

4. Stir together lime gelatin and ½ cup boiling water 1 minute or until gelatin dissolves. Add ½ cup cold water; pour over lemon gelatin in prepared molds, and chill 30 minutes or until firm.

5. Stir together berry blue gelatin and ½ cup boiling water 1 minute or until gelatin dissolves. Add ½ cup cold water; pour over lime gelatin in prepared molds, and chill 30 minutes or until firm.

6. Unmold gelatin by dipping molds in hot water for a couple of seconds. Dry off molds, and turn out gelatins onto a serving dish.

fruity gelatin flowers

MAKES 9 SERVINGS   Hands-On Time: 30 min.   Total Time: 4 hours, 30 min.

1 (3-oz.) package lime-flavored
    gelatin

2/3 cup boiling water

4 (8- x 4-inch) disposable loaf pans

1 (3-oz.) package lemon-flavored
    gelatin

1 (3-oz.) package orange-flavored
    gelatin

1 (3-oz.) package raspberry or cherry-
    flavored gelatin

1. Stir together lime-flavored gelatin and 2/3 cup boiling water 2 minutes or until gelatin dissolves; pour into 1 loaf pan. Repeat process with remaining gelatin and loaf pans. Chill 4 hours or until set.

2. Unmold gelatin onto a clean surface by dipping bottom half of pans in several inches of hot water 2 seconds to loosen. Flip gelatin out onto large plate. Cut lime-flavored gelatin into 18 leaves using a 1-inch cutter. Cut lemon-, orange-, and raspberry-flavored gelatin into 15 petals using a 1-inch cutter and 3 circles using a 1/2-inch cutter.

3. Create flowers on a large serving platter, arranging centers with petals. Arrange leaves around each flower. Chill until ready to serve.

simply smart

The perfect treat for a kids' party, these fruity gellies turn snack time into a fun art project!

cranberry parfaits

MAKES 6 SERVINGS   Hands-On Time: 20 min.   Total Time: 2 hours, 20 min.

. . . .

Serve this ruby-hued dessert as a light ending to a holiday feast.

2 cups fresh or frozen (thawed) cranberries

2 cups miniature marshmallows

¾ cup granulated sugar

2 cups chopped apples (2 medium)

1 cup frozen whipped topping, thawed

2 (3-oz.) packages cream cheese, softened

⅓ cup canned cream of coconut (not coconut milk)

2 Tbsp. powdered sugar

Garnish: sugar-coated cranberries

1. Pulse cranberries in a food processor until chopped. In large bowl, mix cranberries, marshmallows, and granulated sugar, stirring gently. Cover; chill at least 2 hours.

2. Fold apples and whipped topping into cranberry mixture. Spoon into 6 (4-oz.) parfait glasses, filling three-fourths full. In a medium bowl, beat cream cheese, cream of coconut, and powdered sugar at medium speed with an electric mixer until smooth. Top parfaits with cream cheese mixture.

pistachio-strawberry trifles

MAKES 6 SERVINGS   Hands-On Time: 18 min.   Total Time: 1 hour, 41 min.

Choose a green pistachio ice cream or gelato for the most colorful presentation. Wrap and freeze remaining cake to use in other trifles, or crumble and combine with frosting to make cake pops.

1 (16.25-oz.) package white cake mix
3 cups sliced fresh strawberries
¼ cup sugar
2 Tbsp. orange liqueur
4 cups pistachio ice cream or gelato
¼ cup chopped pistachios

1. Preheat oven to 350°. Prepare cake mix according to package directions for a 13- x 9-inch pan. Cool completely in pan on a wire rack (about 1 hour). Cut half of cake into 1-inch cubes. Reserve or freeze remaining cake for another use.

2. Combine strawberries, sugar, and liqueur in a medium bowl. Let stand 30 minutes, stirring occasionally, or until sugar is dissolved.

3. Layer half of cake cubes in each of 6 (8-oz.) glasses. Top with half of strawberry mixture. Top with a scoop of pistachio ice cream. Repeat layers. Sprinkle with pistachios.

sweetheart ice-cream sandwiches

MAKES 12 SERVINGS   Hands-On Time: 30 min.   Total Time: 1 hour, 11 min.

Ice-cream sandwiches are so easy to make in just minutes with cookie dough mix and store-bought ice cream! Decorate with pink and red sprinkles, and you'll be serving Sweetheart Ice-Cream Sandwiches in no time at all!

2 (17.5-oz.) pouches sugar cookie mix

¼ cup all-purpose flour

1 cup butter, softened

2 large eggs

Rose pink food coloring paste

2 cups strawberry ice cream, softened slightly

½ cup pink, red, and white candy sprinkles

1. Preheat oven to 350°. In medium bowl, stir cookie mix, flour, butter, and eggs until soft dough forms. Tint dough pink with food coloring; knead until blended. On a lightly floured surface, roll dough to ¼-inch thickness. Cut with a 3-inch heart-shaped cutter and place on ungreased baking sheets.

2. Bake at 350° for 11 to 13 minutes or until set. Cool on baking sheets 5 minutes. Transfer to wire racks, and cool completely (about 30 minutes).

3. Scoop strawberry ice cream evenly on flat sides of half of cookies; top with remaining cookies, flat sides down. Roll sides of sandwiches in sprinkles. Serve immediately or freeze until ready to serve.

peach melba
ice-cream sandwiches

MAKES 12 SERVINGS   Hands-On Time: 35 min.   Total Time: 4 hours, 11 min.

These cool treats are packed with pops of peach pieces and swirled with fresh raspberries.

1 (16-oz.) package refrigerated ready-to-bake sugar cookie dough
3 Tbsp. pink sprinkles
1 cup frozen raspberries, thawed
2 Tbsp. seedless raspberry jam
Parchment paper
6 cups vanilla ice cream, softened slightly
1 (15¼-oz.) can sliced peaches in heavy syrup, drained and cut into ½-inch pieces

1. Preheat oven to 350°. Shape dough into 24 balls, and roll in sprinkles, coating completely. Place 2 inches apart on ungreased baking sheets. Flatten balls to ½-inch thickness with bottom of a glass. Bake cookies at 350° for 11 to 13 minutes or until set. Cool on baking sheets 5 minutes. Transfer to wire racks, and cool completely (about 30 minutes).

2. Mash raspberries and jam with a fork in a small bowl.

3. Line bottom and sides of a 13- x 9-inch pan with parchment paper, allowing 2 to 3 inches to extend over sides. Gently combine ice cream and peaches; add raspberry mixture, and stir until swirled. Spread mixture evenly into prepared pan. Cover and freeze 3 hours or until very firm.

4. Use parchment paper to lift out of pan. Cut ice cream into 12 circles with a 2¾-inch round cutter. Place 1 ice-cream round between 2 cookies. Freeze until ready to serve.

strawberry lemonade ice-cream cupcakes

MAKES 12 SERVINGS   Hands-On Time: 40 min.   Total Time: 2 hours, 50 min.

These pretty pink-and-yellow ice-cream cupcakes are perfect for a festive summer occasion.

1 (2.9-oz.) package lemon cook-and-serve pudding mix

Paper baking cups

1 (15.25-oz.) package lemon cake mix

1/4 cup vegetable oil

2 large eggs

1/4 tsp. lemon yellow food coloring paste, divided

4 cups strawberry ice cream

1 (8-oz.) container frozen whipped topping, thawed

1/8 tsp. rose food coloring paste

1. Prepare lemon pudding according to package directions. Transfer pudding to a medium bowl; place heavy-duty plastic wrap directly on warm pudding (to prevent a film from forming). Chill 2 hours. (Mixture will thicken as it cools.)

2. Preheat oven to 350°. Place paper baking cups in a 12-cup muffin pan. Beat 1 1/3 cups cake mix (reserve remaining cake mix for another use), 1/2 cup water, oil, eggs, and 1/8 tsp. yellow food coloring at low speed with an electric mixer 30 seconds. Increase speed to medium, and beat 2 minutes. Spoon batter into prepared cups, filling two-thirds full.

3. Bake at 350° for 15 to 18 minutes or until a wooden pick inserted in center comes out clean. Cool completely in pans.

4. Scoop 1/3 cup ice cream onto each cupcake; freeze.

5. Whisk together lemon pudding and whipped topping; divide mixture in half, and place in separate bowls. Stir rose food coloring into 1 bowl of pudding mixture; stir remaining 1/8 tsp. yellow food coloring into other bowl. Spoon pudding mixtures into each of 2 zip-top plastic freezer bags (do not seal). Snip 1 corner of bags to make a small hole. Pipe pudding mixtures alternately onto ice cream, working 2 at a time; cover and freeze 15 minutes or until set. Keep frozen until ready to serve.

Step 5

Step 6

Step 6

mini brownie
baked alaskas

MAKES 4 SERVINGS   Hands-On Time: 40 min.   Total Time: 4 hours

1 cup raspberry sherbet, slightly
    softened

1⅓ cups vanilla ice cream, slightly
    softened

Wax paper

Unsweetened cocoa

1¼ cups bittersweet chocolate
    morsels

⅓ cup butter

1⅔ cups sugar

2 large eggs

¾ cup all-purpose flour

⅛ tsp. baking powder

⅛ tsp. salt

1¼ tsp. vanilla

Parchment paper

Meringue

meringue

Beat 2 egg whites, ¼ tsp. cream of tartar, and ¼ tsp. vanilla with electric mixer at high speed until foamy. Gradually add ¼ cup sugar, 1 Tbsp. at a time, beating at high speed until stiff peaks form and sugar is dissolved. Do not underbeat.

1. Divide sherbet into 4 lightly greased (6-oz.) ramekins, pressing firmly up sides of cups. Divide ice cream into cups, spreading to edge and pressing firmly. Cover and freeze 2 hours or until firm.

2. Preheat oven to 350°. Line bottom and sides of a lightly greased 8-inch square pan with wax paper. Grease wax paper, and sprinkle with cocoa.

3. In large glass bowl, microwave chocolate morsels and butter at HIGH 1 to 2 minutes or until melted, stirring every 30 seconds. Whisk in sugar. Add eggs, one at a time, stirring until blended. Gradually add flour, baking powder, and salt, whisking just until blended. Stir in vanilla. Spread batter in pan.

4. Bake at 350° for 20 to 25 minutes or until set. Cool completely, about 40 minutes.

5. Line a baking sheet with parchment paper. Using a 3¼-inch round cutter, cut out 4 brownie rounds; place on baking sheet about 2 inches apart. Remove ice cream cups from freezer. Run small metal spatula around edge of each cup to loosen ice cream. Immediately turn each cup upside down onto a brownie round; remove cups. Freeze ice cream-topped brownies until ready to use.

6. Preheat oven to 450°. Using an offset spatula, spread meringue over ice cream-topped brownies, sealing meringue to bottom edge of brownies. Bake 3 to 4 minutes or lightly toast with a kitchen torch. Serve immediately.

strawberry semifreddo shortcake

MAKES 16 SERVINGS   Hands-On Time: 30 min.   Total Time: 5 hours, 45 min.

2 (3-oz.) packages soft ladyfingers
2 pt. strawberry ice cream, softened
1 pt. strawberry sorbet, softened
1 pt. fresh strawberries, hulled
2 Tbsp. powdered sugar
½ (7-oz.) jar marshmallow crème
1 cup heavy cream

1. Arrange ladyfingers on bottom and around sides of a lightly greased 9-inch springform pan. (Reserve any remaining ladyfingers for another use.) Spread strawberry ice cream over ladyfingers, and freeze 30 minutes.

2. Spread softened strawberry sorbet over ice cream. Freeze 30 minutes.

3. Process strawberries and powdered sugar in a food processor 1 minute or until pureed. Reserve ¼ cup mixture. Whisk remaining strawberry mixture into marshmallow crème until well blended.

4. Beat heavy cream at high speed with an electric mixer until stiff peaks form. Fold into marshmallow mixture. Pour over sorbet in pan. Drizzle reserved ¼ cup strawberry mixture over top, and gently swirl with a paring knife. Freeze 4 hours or until firm. Let ice-cream cake stand at room temperature 15 minutes before serving.

Note: We tested with Blue Bell Strawberry Ice Cream and Häagen-Dazs Strawberry Sorbet.

simply smart

Although soft ladyfingers are the best dessert, you can also use the crispy variety of lady-fingers; just cut them to fit around the sides and bottom of the spring-form pan.

coconut-raspberry-mango sorbet cake

MAKES 16 SERVINGS   Hands-On Time: 20 min.   Total Time: 8 hours, 50 min.

Take a trip to the tropics with this rich coconut cake layered with bright mango and raspberry sorbets and topped with a cloud of whipped topping. Top that with even more coconut!

1 (16.25-oz.) package white cake mix

Water, oil, and egg whites called for on cake mix box

Parchment paper

2 (8-oz.) containers frozen whipped topping, thawed

Disposable decorating bag

4 cups mango sorbet, softened

4 cups raspberry sorbet, softened

1 (7-oz.) can sweetened flaked coconut

1. Preheat oven to 350°. Prepare cake mix according to package directions using water, oil, and egg whites. Pour batter into 3 greased and parchment paper-lined 9-inch round cake pans.

2. Bake at 350° for 20 minutes or until a wooden pick inserted in center comes out clean. Cool in pans on wire racks 10 minutes; remove from pans to wire racks, and cool completely (about 1 hour).

3. Line bottom and sides of a 9- x 3-inch springform pan with plastic wrap, allowing wrap to extend over sides. Place one cake layer on bottom of pan. Spoon 1¼ cups whipped topping into a disposable decorating bag fitted with a round tip. Pipe a ring around the edge of the cake.

4. Spread mango sorbet on cake in an even layer. Top with second cake layer; pipe a ring of whipped topping around the edge. Spread raspberry sorbet on cake in an even layer. Top with remaining cake layer. Cover with plastic wrap, and freeze 6 hours or overnight.

5. Unmold cake, and remove plastic wrap; trim edges if desired. Place on a serving plate. Frost top and sides of cake with remaining whipped topping. Sprinkle top and sides with coconut. Freeze 1 hour or until firm.

mint-chocolate chip ice-cream cake

MAKES 10 TO 12 SERVINGS

Hands-On Time: 30 min.   Total Time: 10 hours, 30 min., including ganache

Parchment paper

½ cup butter, softened

¾ cup sugar

1 large egg

1 tsp. vanilla extract

1 cup all-purpose flour

⅓ cup unsweetened cocoa

1 tsp. baking soda

¾ cup hot strong brewed coffee

1 tsp. white vinegar

½ gal. mint-chocolate chip ice cream, softened

10 chocolate wafers, coarsely crushed

Chocolate Ganache

Garnishes: whipped cream, thin chocolate mints

chocolate ganache

Microwave 1 (4-oz.) semisweet chocolate baking bar, chopped, and 4 Tbsp. whipping cream in a microwave-safe bowl at HIGH 1 minute or until melted, stirring at 30-second intervals. Stir in up to 4 Tbsp. additional cream for desired consistency. Use immediately.

1. Preheat oven to 350°. Grease and flour 3 (8-inch) round cake pans. Line with parchment paper.

2. Beat butter and sugar at medium speed with a heavy-duty electric stand mixer until creamy. Add egg, beating just until blended. Beat in vanilla. Combine flour, cocoa, and baking soda in a separate bowl. Add to butter mixture alternately with coffee, beating until blended. Stir in vinegar. Pour into prepared pans.

3. Bake at 350° for 12 to 14 minutes or until a wooden pick inserted in center comes out clean. Cool in pans on wire racks 10 minutes. Remove from pans to wire racks, peel off parchment paper, and cool completely (about 1 hour).

4. Place 1 cake layer in a 9-inch springform pan. Top with one-third of ice cream (about 2⅓ cups); sprinkle with half of crushed wafers. Repeat layers once. Top with remaining cake layer and ice cream. Freeze 8 to 12 hours.

5. Remove cake from springform pan, and place on a cake stand or plate. Prepare Chocolate Ganache, and spread over top of ice-cream cake. Let stand 15 minutes before serving.

Resource Note: We tested with Andes Crème de Menthe Thins.

Beyond the Batter Resources

You can find many of the basic supplies you'll need to make your desserts at home-goods stores like Hobby Lobby, Party City, Target, and Walmart. However, here are the names of a few websites where you can buy specialty supplies that will allow you to give your treats that extra-special touch.

1 **Candied Flowers**
Sweet Estelle (www.sweetestelle.com)
Wilton (www.wilton.com)

2 **Cake Toppers**
Bake It Pretty (www.bakeitpretty.com)
Walmart (www.walmart.com)

3 **Colorful Cutlery**
Hobby Lobby (www.hobbylobby.com)
Party City (www.partycity.com)
Wally's Party Factory
(www. wallyspartyfactory.com)

4 **Sprinkles**
Party City (www.partycity.com)
Target (www.target.com)

5 **Craft Sticks**
Hobby Lobby (www.hobbylobby.com)
Party City (www.partycity.com)

6 **Striped Straws**
Bake It Pretty (www.bakeitpretty. com)
Target (www.target.com)
The Cupcake Social
(www.thecupcakesocial.com)

7 **Candy Pearls**
Hobby Lobby (www.hobbylobby.com)
The Cupcake Social
(www.thecupcakesocial.com)
Walmart (www.walmart.com)

8 **Birthday Candles**
Party City (www.partycity.com)
Target (www.target.com)

9 **Food Coloring**
Target (www.target.com)
Wilton (www.wilton.com)

10 **Cupcake Wrappers/Liners**
Bake It Pretty (www.bakeitpretty.com)
Hobby Lobby (www.hobbylobby.com)
Wilton (www.wilton.com)

index

metric equivalents

The recipes that appear in this cookbook use the standard U.S. method for measuring liquid and dry or solid ingredients (teaspoons, tablespoons, and cups). The information in the following charts is provided to help cooks outside the United States successfully use these recipes. All equivalents are approximate.

Metric Equivalents for Different Types of Ingredients

A standard cup measure of a dry or solid ingredient will vary in weight depending on the type of ingredient. A standard cup of liquid is the same volume for any type of liquid. Use the following chart when converting standard cup measures to grams (weight) or milliliters (volume).

Standard Cup	Fine Powder (ex. flour)	Grain (ex. rice)	Granular (ex. sugar)	Liquid Solids (ex. butter)	Liquid (ex. milk)
1	140 g	150 g	190 g	200 g	240 ml
3/4	105 g	113 g	143 g	150 g	180 ml
2/3	93 g	100 g	125 g	133 g	160 ml
1/2	70 g	75 g	95 g	100 g	120 ml
1/3	47 g	50 g	63 g	67 g	80 ml
1/4	35 g	38 g	48 g	50 g	60 ml
1/8	18 g	19 g	24 g	25 g	30 ml

Useful Equivalents for Liquid Ingredients by Volume

1/4 tsp				=	1 ml
1/2 tsp				=	2 ml
1 tsp				=	5 ml
3 tsp	= 1 Tbsp		= 1/2 fl oz	=	15 ml
	2 Tbsp	= 1/8 cup	= 1 fl oz	=	30 ml
	4 Tbsp	= 1/4 cup	= 2 fl oz	=	60 ml
	5 1/3 Tbsp	= 1/3 cup	= 3 fl oz	=	80 ml
	8 Tbsp	= 1/2 cup	= 4 fl oz	=	120 ml
	10 2/3 Tbsp	= 2/3 cup	= 5 fl oz	=	160 ml
	12 Tbsp	= 3/4 cup	= 6 fl oz	=	180 ml
	16 Tbsp	= 1 cup	= 8 fl oz	=	240 ml
	1 pt	= 2 cups	= 16 fl oz	=	480 ml
	1 qt	= 4 cups	= 32 fl oz	=	960 ml
			33 fl oz	= 1000 ml	= 1 l

Useful Equivalents for Dry Ingredients by Weight

(To convert ounces to grams, multiply the number of ounces by 30.)

1 oz	=	1/16 lb	=	30 g
4 oz	=	1/4 lb	=	120 g
8 oz	=	1/2 lb	=	240 g
12 oz	=	3/4 lb	=	360 g
16 oz	=	1 lb	=	480 g

Useful Equivalents for Length

(To convert inches to centimeters, multiply the number of inches by 2.5.)

1 in		=	2.5 cm	
6 in	= 1/2 ft	=	15 cm	
12 in	= 1 ft	=	30 cm	
36 in	= 3 ft = 1 yd	=	90 cm	
40 in		=	100 cm	= 1 m

Useful Equivalents for Cooking/Oven Temperatures

	Fahrenheit	Celsius	Gas Mark
Freeze water	32° F	0° C	
Room temperature	68° F	20° C	
Boil water	212° F	100° C	
Bake	325° F	160° C	3
	350° F	180° C	4
	375° F	190° C	5
	400° F	200° C	6
	425° F	220° C	7
	450° F	230° C	8
Broil			Grill

ISBN-13: 978-0-8487-4304-8
ISBN-10: 0-8487-4304-0
Library of Congress Control Number:
2013957462

Printed in the United States of America
First Printing 2014

Oxmoor House

Vice President, Brand Publishing:
  Laura Sappington
Editorial Director: Leah McLaughlin
Creative Director: Felicity Keane
Brand Manager: Katie McHugh
Senior Editor: Rebecca Brennan
Managing Editor: Elizabeth Tyler Austin
Assistant Managing Editor: Jeanne de Lathouder

ColorCakes

Editor: Allison E. Cox
Art Director: Christopher Rhoads
Project Editor: Emily Chappell Connolly
Assistant Designer: Allison Sperando Potter
Junior Designer: Maribeth Jones
Executive Food Director: Grace Parisi
Assistant Test Kitchen Manager: Alyson
  Moreland Haynes
Recipe Developers and Testers: Wendy Ball,
  R.D.; Tamara Goldis, R.D.; Stefanie Maloney;
  Callie Nash; Karen Rankin; Leah Van Deren
Food Stylists: Victoria E. Cox, Margaret Monroe
  Dickey, Catherine Crowell Steele
Photography Director: Jim Bathie
Senior Photographer: Hélène Dujardin
Senior Photo Stylist: Kay E. Clarke
Photo Stylist: Mindi Shapiro Levine
Assistant Photo Stylist: Mary Louise Menendez
Associate Production Manager: Amy Mangus
Assistant Production Manager: Diane Rose Keener

Contributors

Designer: Anna Christian
Compositor: Frances Higginbotham
Recipe Developers and Testers: Gwynn
  Galvin, Erica Bruce, Yvonne Ruperti, Jan Smith
Copy Editors: Rebecca Henderson, Carmine Loper
Indexer: Mary Ann Laurens
Fellows: Ali Carruba, Elizabeth Laseter, Amy
  Pinney, Madison Taylor Pozzo, Deanna Sakal,
  April Smitherman, Megan Thompson,
  Tonya West
Food Stylists: Stephana Bottom,
  Ana Price Kelly
Photographer: Ellen Silverman
Photo Stylists: Megan Hedgpeth,
  Lydia DeGaris Pursell

Time Home Entertainment Inc.

Publisher: Jim Childs
Vice President, Brand & Digital Strategy:
  Steven Sandonato
Executive Director, Marketing Services:
  Carol Pittard
Executive Director, Retail & Special Sales:
  Tom Mifsud
Director, Bookazine Development &
  Marketing: Laura Adam
Executive Publishing Director: Joy Butts
Publishing Director: Megan Pearlman
Finance Director: Glenn Buonocore
Associate General Counsel: Helen Wan